# THE WAR TO END WARS 1914–1919

## GCSE Modern World History for Edexcel

Steve Waugh
John Wright

**Hodder Murray**
A MEMBER OF THE HODDER HEADLINE GROUP

# In memory of Lance Corporal John Spurr, 1898–1916

This high-quality material is endorsed by Edexcel and has been through a rigorous quality assurance programme to ensure that it is a suitable companion to the specification for both learners and teachers. This does not mean that its contents will be used verbatim when setting examinations nor is it to be read as being the official specification – a copy of which is available at www.edexcel.org.uk.

The Publishers would like to thank the following for permission to reproduce copyright material:

**Photo credits**
**Cover** *l* Topical Press Agency/Getty Images, *r* © Hulton-Deutsch Collection/CORBIS; **p.7** The Art Archive/Imperial War Museum; **p.9** Popperfoto.com; **p.11** Mary Evans Picture Library; **p.12** *t* The Art Archive/Imperial War Museum, *b* © Courtesy of the Council, National Army Museum, London/The Bridgeman Art Library; **p.14** Getty Images; **p.15** The Art Archive/Imperial War Museum; **p.16** Imperial War Museum, London (Q49104); **p.17** The Art Archive; **p.19** Imperial War Museum, London; **p.20** *t* Imperial War Museum, London (Q87923), *b* Imperial War Museum, London (Q6049); **p.22** *l* Imperial War Museum, London (Q872), *r* Imperial War Museum, London (Q583); **p.25** Getty Images; **p.27** *t* The Art Archive/Imperial War Museum, *b* Imperial War Museum, London (Q51438); **p.29** Imperial War Museum, London (C02246); **p.30** Imperial War Museum, London (Q4510); **p.32** Imperial War Museum, London; **p.35** Imperial War Museum, London (Q33169); **p.36** *t* Popperfoto.com, *cl* Ann Ronan Picture Library/HIP/TopFoto, *cr & b* ullstein bild; **p.39** Imperial War Museum, London (Q63667); **p.40** The Art Archive/Australian War Memorial; **p.41** The Robert Hunt Library; **p.43** © Corbis; **p.44** © Corbis; **p.46** Imperial War Museum, London (Q11586); **p.47** TopFoto; **p.51** TopFoto; **p.52** Library and Archives Canada (C-080027); **p.53** W.K. Haselden, Daily Mirror, 10 May 1915, © Mirrorpix (photo: British Cartoon Archive, University of Kent); **p.54** The Illustrated London News Picture Library; **p.55** *t* Getty Images, *b* Imperial War Museum, London; **p.57** Topfoto; **p.58** *l* The Illustrated London News Picture Library, *r* © Bettmann/Corbis; **p.61** *t* David King Collection, *c* Popperfoto.com, *b* RIA Novosti; **p.62** Getty Images; **p.63** David King Collection; **p.64** *t* © Corbis, *b* Culver Pictures; **p.65** *t* Getty Images; **p.67** © Corbis; **p.68** *t* The Art Archive/Imperial War Museum, *b* Getty Images; **p.69** *t* Getty Images, *b* Imperial War Museum, London (Q56794); **p.70** ullstein bild; **p.71** The Art Archive/Imperial War Museum; **p.73** © Bettmann/Corbis; **p.74** *l* ullstein bild, *tr* Library of Congress, Prints and Photographs Division (LC-USZC4-4963), *br* The Art Archive/Culver Pictures; **p.79** © Bettmann/Corbis; **p.80** David Low, Evening Standard, 3 July 1919, © Associated Newspapers/Solo Syndication (photo: British Cartoon Archive, University of Kent); **p.83** The Art Archive/Eileen Tweedy; **p.86** *l* W.K. Haselden, Daily Mirror, 24 June 1919, © Mirrorpix (photo: British Cartoon Archive, University of Kent), *r* © Hulton-Deutsch Collection/Corbis; **p.87** Mary Evans Picture Library.

**Acknowledgements**
**p.5** Edexcel Limited, *June 2006 Papers 1 and 2 1334 GCSE Modern World History*; **p.18** *A* David Lloyd George, *Memoirs*, Odhams Press Limited, 1938, *B* Robin Lobban, *The First World War*, Oxford University Press, 1982; **p.25** *C* Josh Brooman, *The Great War*, Longman, 1985, *E* Philip Warner, *Field Marshal Haig*, The Bodley Head Ltd, 1991, *F* Steve Waugh, *Essential Modern World History*, Nelson Thornes, 2001; **p.32** *A* Craig Mair, *Britain at War*, John Murray, 1982; **p.41** *D* Geoffrey Regan, *The Guinness Book of Military Blunders*, Guinness World Records Limited, 1991, *E* Michael Hickey, *Gallipoli*, John Murray, 1995; **p.42** *A* 'And the band played Waltzing Matilda' by Eric Bogle © Larrikin Music Publishing. International Copyright Secured. All rights reserved. Lyrics reproduced with permission; **p.44** *B* Arthur Guy Empey, *Over the Top*, 1917 (University Press of the Pacific, 2001); **p.45** *C* Wilfred Owen, 'Dulce et decorum est'; **p.52** *D* Brig Gen Sir James E. Edmonds, *Military Operations: France and Belgium, 1918*, 1947 (Imperial War Museum, 1992); **p.59** *A* Matthew Holden, *War in the Trenches*, Wayland, 1973; **p.70** *A* Nigel Kelly, *The First World War*, Heinemann, 1989; **p.72** *E* Gen Erich Ludendorff, *My War Memories*, 1919 (Naval and Military Press, 2005); **p.75** mark scheme Edexcel.

Every effort has been made to trace all copyright holders, but if any have been inadvertently overlooked the Publishers will be pleased to make the necessary arrangements at the first opportunity.

Although every effort has been made to ensure that website addresses are correct at time of going to press, Hodder Murray cannot be held responsible for the content of any website mentioned in this book. It is sometimes possible to find a relocated web page by typing in the address of the home page for a website in the URL window of your browser.

Hodder Headline's policy is to use papers that are natural, renewable and recyclable products and made from wood grown in sustainable forests. The logging and manufacturing processes are expected to conform to the environmental regulations of the country of origin.

Orders: please contact Bookpoint Ltd, 130 Milton Park, Abingdon, Oxon OX14 4SB. Telephone: +44 (0)1235 827720. Fax: +44 (0)1235 400454. Lines are open 9.00–5.00, Monday to Saturday, with a 24-hour message answering service. Visit our website at www.hoddereducation.co.uk

© Steve Waugh and John Wright 2007
First published in 2007
by Hodder Murray, an imprint of Hodder Education,
a member of the Hodder Headline Group,
an Hachette Livre UK company
338 Euston Road
London NW1 3BH

Impression number    5  4  3  2  1
Year                 2010  2009  2008  2007

All rights reserved. Apart from any use permitted under UK copyright law, no part of this publication may be reproduced or transmitted in any form or by any means, electronic or mechanical, including photocopying and recording, or held within any information storage and retrieval system, without permission in writing from the publisher or under licence from the Copyright Licensing Agency Limited. Further details of such licences (for reprographic reproduction) may be obtained from the Copyright Licensing Agency Limited, Saffron House, 6–10 Kirby Street, London EC1N 8TS.

Typeset in 12 pt Garamond by Fakenham Photosetting Ltd
Artwork by Tony Jones, Tony Randell and Steve Smith
Printed in Italy

A catalogue record for this title is available from the British Library

ISBN: 978 0 340 93975 8

# Contents

| | |
|---|---|
| **Acknowledgements** | 2 |
| **Introduction** | 4 |
| **Chapter 1 The failure of the Schlieffen Plan** | **7** |
| • Why did war break out? | 8 |
| • What was the Schlieffen Plan? | 10 |
| • Why did the Schlieffen Plan fail? | 12 |
| • Why was the Battle of the Marne, 5–19 September, decisive? | 14 |
| • Why was there a race for the sea? | 15 |
| • What was the situation by the end of 1914? | 16 |
| • Examination practice | 18 |
| **Chapter 2 Stalemate on the Western Front, 1915–17** | **19** |
| • What was the trench system? | 20 |
| • What was it like for the soldiers in the trenches? | 22 |
| • Why was there a stalemate for three years? | 24 |
| • What part did Haig play in the stalemate? | 25 |
| • Why was there no breakthrough at the Somme and at Passchendaele? | 26 |
| • Examination practice | 30 |
| **Chapter 3 The war at sea and Gallipoli** | **33** |
| • How did the German navy threaten Britain? | 34 |
| • What were the key events in the North Sea, 1914–15? | 35 |
| • What was the importance of the Battle of Jutland? | 36 |
| • Why did the Allies launch the Gallipoli campaign? | 38 |
| • Why did the Gallipoli campaign fail? | 40 |
| • Examination practice | 42 |
| **Chapter 4 The impact of technology on the war** | **43** |
| • How was gas used on the Western Front? | 44 |
| • How were tanks used on the Western Front? | 47 |
| • Examination practice | 50 |
| • How did U-boats threaten Britain? | 53 |
| • How was Britain able to overcome the threat of the U-boats? | 54 |
| • What changes took place in the war in the air? | 56 |
| • Examination practice | 58 |
| **Chapter 5 The defeat of Germany, 1917–18** | **59** |
| • Why did Russia withdraw from the war in 1917? | 60 |
| • Why and with what effect did the USA enter the war in 1917? | 64 |
| • What was the Spring Offensive and why did it fail? | 68 |
| • How and why did Germany collapse in 1918? | 70 |
| • Examination practice | 74 |
| **Chapter 6 The peace settlement, 1919–20** | **77** |
| • What were the aims of the 'Big Three'? | 78 |
| • What were the main terms of the Treaty of Versailles? | 80 |
| • Why were many Germans opposed to the treaty? | 84 |
| • What were the other main peace treaties? | 85 |
| • Examination practice | 86 |
| **Revision activities** | 88 |
| **Glossary** | 94 |
| **Index** | 96 |

# Introduction

## About the book
This book is designed to help support the study of *The War to End Wars, 1914–19* depth study. It covers the key developments in the First World War (1914–18) and the peace treaties that followed. In the study you will learn:

- why a cunning German plan to win the war quickly failed in 1914
- how British and German troops played football on Christmas Day 1914
- why the two sides were locked in a stalemate for three years
- how 20,000 British troops were killed on the morning of 1 July 1916
- why a German U-boat sank a passenger liner in 1915
- why Sir Douglas Haig was nicknamed the 'Butcher of the Somme'
- how Allied troops ended up on beaches in Gallipoli in 1915
- why water carriers became known as tanks.

Each chapter in this book:

- contains activities – some help to develop the historical skills you will need, others are exam-style questions that give you the opportunity to practise exam skills
- gives step-by-step guidance, model answers and advice on how to answer particular question types
- highlights glossary terms in bold the first time they appear
- is covered in a revision section at the end of the book.

## About the course
During this course you must study two outline studies, two depth studies and two coursework units. There are two written exam papers.

- In Paper 1 you have two hours to answer questions on two outline studies.
- In Paper 2 you have one and three-quarter hours to answer questions on two depth studies.

## Depth Studies (Paper 2)
Depth Studies give you the opportunity to study a much shorter period in greater depth. As well as the depth study on *The War to End Wars, 1914–19* you will also study another one as part of this course. For example:

- Depression and the New Deal: The USA, 1929–41
- The Russian Revolution, *c.*1910–1924
- The World at War, 1938–45
- Conflict in Vietnam, 1963–75
- The End of Apartheid in South Africa, 1982–94

The Depth Studies are assessed through Paper 2. Paper 2 is a test of:

- knowledge and understanding of a shorter period in history
- the ability to answer four different types of source questions.

In order to answer Paper 2 questions successfully, you will need to have generic and question-specific source skills.

- 'Generic' means your ability to examine the nature, origins and purpose of sources.
- 'Question specific' refers to the four different types of source questions. These are:
  – inference
  – cross-referencing
  – utility
  – synthesis (the ability to discuss an interpretation).

## Depth study questions

In the examination you will be given six sources and have to answer four questions. Below are the questions (without the sources) on the depth study for the June 2006 exam.

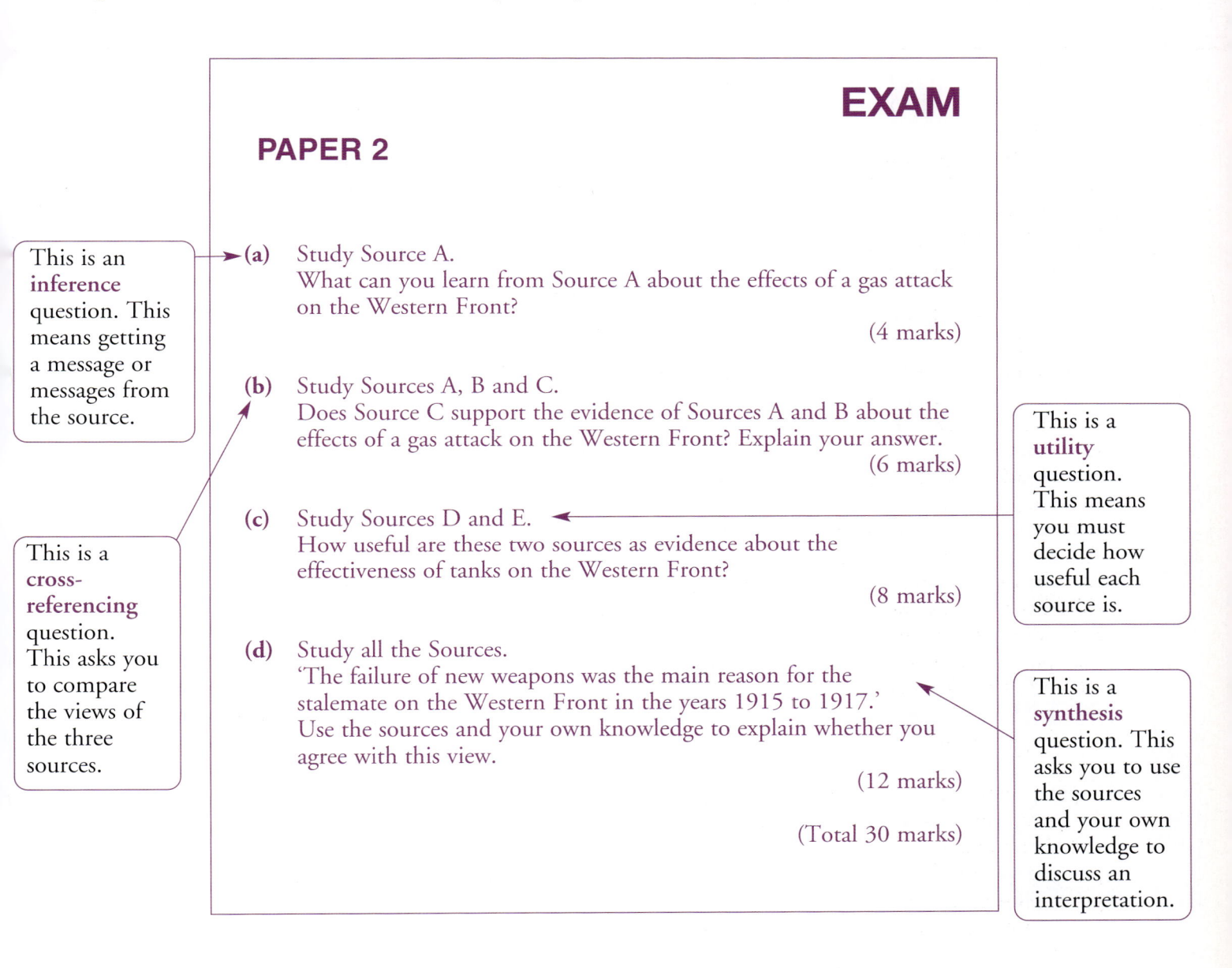

**EXAM PAPER 2**

(a) Study Source A.
What can you learn from Source A about the effects of a gas attack on the Western Front?
(4 marks)

(b) Study Sources A, B and C.
Does Source C support the evidence of Sources A and B about the effects of a gas attack on the Western Front? Explain your answer.
(6 marks)

(c) Study Sources D and E.
How useful are these two sources as evidence about the effectiveness of tanks on the Western Front?
(8 marks)

(d) Study all the Sources.
'The failure of new weapons was the main reason for the stalemate on the Western Front in the years 1915 to 1917.'
Use the sources and your own knowledge to explain whether you agree with this view.
(12 marks)

(Total 30 marks)

*This is an **inference** question. This means getting a message or messages from the source.*

*This is a **cross-referencing** question. This asks you to compare the views of the three sources.*

*This is a **utility** question. This means you must decide how useful each source is.*

*This is a **synthesis** question. This asks you to use the sources and your own knowledge to discuss an interpretation.*

You will be given step-by-step guidance on how to answer all these questions in the first five chapters. Chapter 6 will give you the opportunity to practise all question types.

## Generic source skills

Look at the four questions on the exam paper on the previous page. You will have to answer each of these four types of question for each of your depth studies in Paper 2. In order to answer these source questions you need to have some basic, general source skills. You need to be confident in examining the NOP of sources as this will help you to answer the questions set out later. NOP stands for:

**N**ature
**O**rigin
**P**urpose

Examining the NOP of sources means asking:

- Who?
- When?
- Why?
- Where?
- What?

Some examples of the type of question NOP encourages you to ask are given below.

### Nature
- What type of source is it? Is it a:

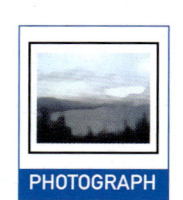

DIARY | LETTER | PHOTOGRAPH
NEWSPAPER REPORT | SPEECH | CARTOON

- How will this influence the utility (usefulness) of the source? For example, photographs can capture only one moment in time but can still be useful.

### Origins
- Who produced the source?
  - What do I know about this person or organisation?
  - Is this person or organisation likely to give a one-sided view of the event? If so, which side do I not get?
- When was the source produced?
  - Is it the evidence of an eyewitness? What are the advantages and disadvantages of eyewitness evidence?
  - Was it written at a later date? Did the person have the benefit of hindsight?
  - What are the advantages and limitations of sources that were written later?
- Under what circumstances or in what situation was the source produced? For example, some sources are written under strict government control and censorship and the person who wrote the source may not have the freedom to write what they genuinely believed.

### Purpose
- Why was the source produced, written, drawn, etc.?
- Is the person trying to make you support one view or one side? For example, cartoons are usually drawn to make fun of people and/or events although some cartoons use humour to get across a serious point.
- Is the source an example of propaganda? If so, what view is it trying to get across? (Be careful, propaganda sources are useful because they provide evidence of the methods used to gain support.)

Chapters 1–6 will help develop these generic source skills using a variety of sources and tasks.

The War to End Wars 1914–1919

# 1 The failure of the Schlieffen Plan

**Source A** From a letter by a British officer to his parents, August 1914

*You must all keep cheerful for my sake and it will not last long before I am back again. The general is convinced that it will not be a long show.*

**Task**

What can you learn about the war from Sources A and B? (This is an inference question. For further guidance, see page 18.)

**Source B** A French infantry regiment being given a rousing send-off by a crowd in 1914

Most people were as convinced as the officer in Source A that the war would be over quickly. After all, the last major European conflict, the Franco-Prussian War of 1870–71, had been relatively short-lived. Indeed, had the German military plan known as the Schlieffen Plan worked, then France and Russia would have been defeated quickly and Britain possibly forced to retreat to the safety of her own shores. The failure of the Schlieffen Plan led to stalemate on the Western Front and a long drawn-out conflict.

This chapter answers the following questions:
- Why did war break out?
- What was the Schlieffen Plan?
- Why did the Schlieffen Plan fail?
- Why was the Battle of the Marne, 5–19 September, decisive?
- Why was there a race for the sea?
- What was the situation by the end of 1914?

## Source skills

In this chapter you will look at inference questions from Paper 2. The inference question is worth four marks. There are also questions throughout the chapter that help you to develop your understanding of the topic. Do remember that in Paper 2 you have to answer questions that examine not only your source skills but also your knowledge and understanding of the topic.

# Why did war break out?

The immediate reason for the outbreak of the First World War in August 1914 was the assassination of the Austrian Archduke Franz Ferdinand in June 1914. However, the cause of the war was mainly due to a build up of rivalry and tension over the preceding 30 years between the Great Powers of Britain, France, Germany, Austria and Russia.

## Tasks

1. Read pages 8–9 and give one reason why each of the Great Powers went to war in 1914.

2. After a class discussion about the reasons for the outbreak of the war, decide what you think was the most important reason. Explain your answer.

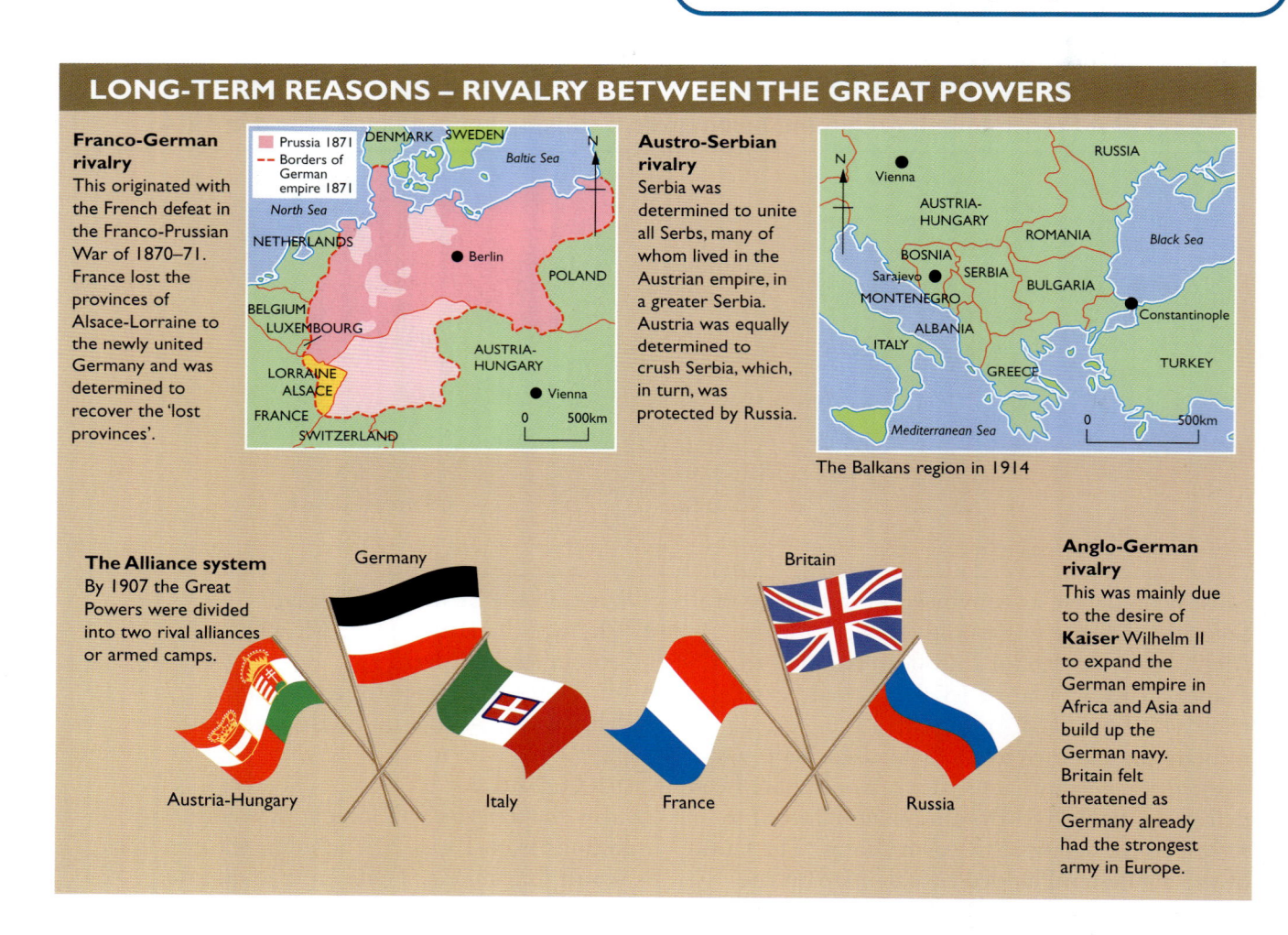

## LONG-TERM REASONS – RIVALRY BETWEEN THE GREAT POWERS

**Franco-German rivalry**
This originated with the French defeat in the Franco-Prussian War of 1870–71. France lost the provinces of Alsace-Lorraine to the newly united Germany and was determined to recover the 'lost provinces'.

**Austro-Serbian rivalry**
Serbia was determined to unite all Serbs, many of whom lived in the Austrian empire, in a greater Serbia. Austria was equally determined to crush Serbia, which, in turn, was protected by Russia.

The Balkans region in 1914

**The Alliance system**
By 1907 the Great Powers were divided into two rival alliances or armed camps.

Germany — Britain
Austria-Hungary — Italy — France — Russia

**Anglo-German rivalry**
This was mainly due to the desire of **Kaiser** Wilhelm II to expand the German empire in Africa and Asia and build up the German navy. Britain felt threatened as Germany already had the strongest army in Europe.

8  The War to End Wars 1914–1919

## SHORT-TERM REASONS – SERIES OF CRISES 1905–13

**1905 Moroccan crisis**
Kaiser Wilhelm II tried, unsuccessfully, to prevent France occupying Morocco. Britain fully supported France. The Kaiser's interference brought France and Britain closer.

**1906 *Dreadnought***
Britain launched a modern battleship, the ***Dreadnought***, which made all previous battleships obsolete. A naval race between Britain and Germany followed, as they competed to build the biggest fleet of modern battleships.

**1908–9 Bosnian crisis**
Austria occupied Bosnia, a province coveted by the Serbs. Serbia, supported by Russia, was furious.

**1911 Moroccan crisis**
Germany sent a gunboat to the Moroccan port of Agadir to force compensation from France for its gaining control of Morocco in 1906. Britain again backed France and the Kaiser had to scale down his demands.

**1912–13 Balkan wars**
In a series of wars against first Turkey and then Bulgaria, Serbia gained a considerable amount of territory and became a much greater threat to Austria.

## The final trigger

An illustration showing the assassination of Franz Ferdinand. On 28 June 1914 the heir to the Austrian throne, Archduke Franz Ferdinand, and his wife Sophie paid a state visit to Sarajevo, the capital of Bosnia. They were shot by Gavrilo Princip, a Serbian terrorist. The murder sparked a series of events that led to the outbreak of war (see below).

**23 July** The Austrians, supported by Germany, delivered a severe **ultimatum** to Serbia.

**28 July** The Serbian reply did not satisfy Austria, which declared war on Serbia.

**29 July** Russia began to **mobilise** its armed forces in support of Serbia.

**1 August** Germany declared war on Russia when Russia refused to halt mobilisation.

**3 August** Germany declared war on France following France's refusal to promise to remain neutral in the conflict between Germany/Austria and Russia.

**4 August** Britain declared war on Germany after the German invasion of Belgium.

The failure of the Schlieffen Plan

# What was the Schlieffen Plan?

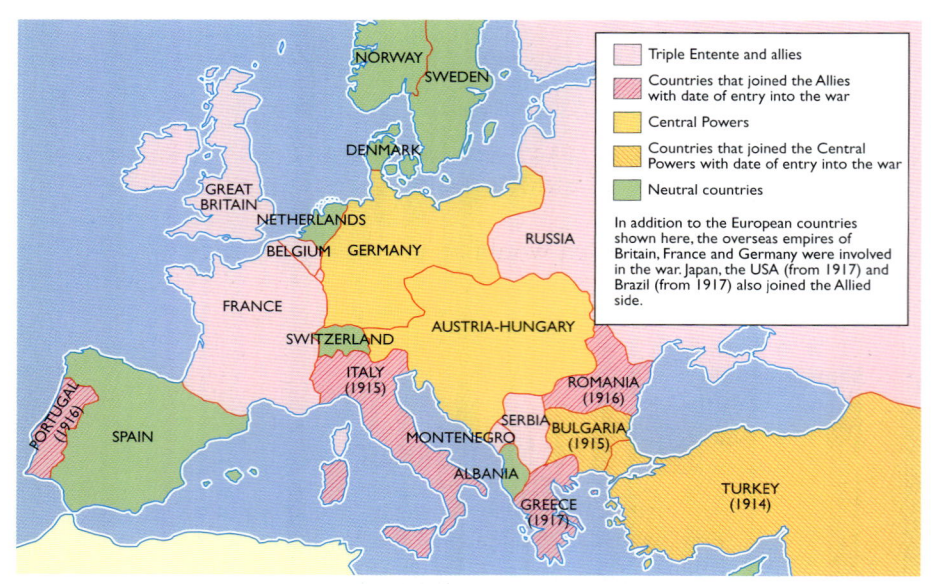

*A map of Europe in 1914 showing the two alliance systems*

## The two sides
The war was fought between the **Central Powers** – Germany and Austria-Hungary – and the **Triple Entente** of Britain, France and Russia (the Allies).

## The Central Powers
Of all the Great Powers, Germany had the largest peacetime army, with over 2 million men, which was well trained, organised and disciplined. Germany was also the only power with a plan to fight a war. Its weakness was its ally, Austria-Hungary. Austria-Hungary had an army of less than 1 million, many of whom were non-Austrians from the Austrian empire and not keen to fight in a war.

## The Triple Entente
Britain was the only country among the Great Powers that did not have **conscription**. It had a small, professional army of about 700,000. In the years before the outbreak of war a **British Expeditionary Force** (**BEF**) was put together that could be quickly transported to France.

France had an army of 1.25 million men but it lacked the organisation and efficiency of its German counterpart and had no real plan, apart from invading Alsace-Lorraine. Russia also had an army of 1.25 million but it was poorly equipped with generally incompetent commanders.

## The Schlieffen Plan
Germany had long feared a war on two fronts, with France to the west and Russia to the east. In 1905 Count von Schlieffen, the Chief of the German General Staff, prepared a plan to avoid having to fight on both fronts at the same time. He believed that due to the terrible state of the country's roads and its inefficient railways, Russia would take about six weeks to mobilise. In the meantime, the German

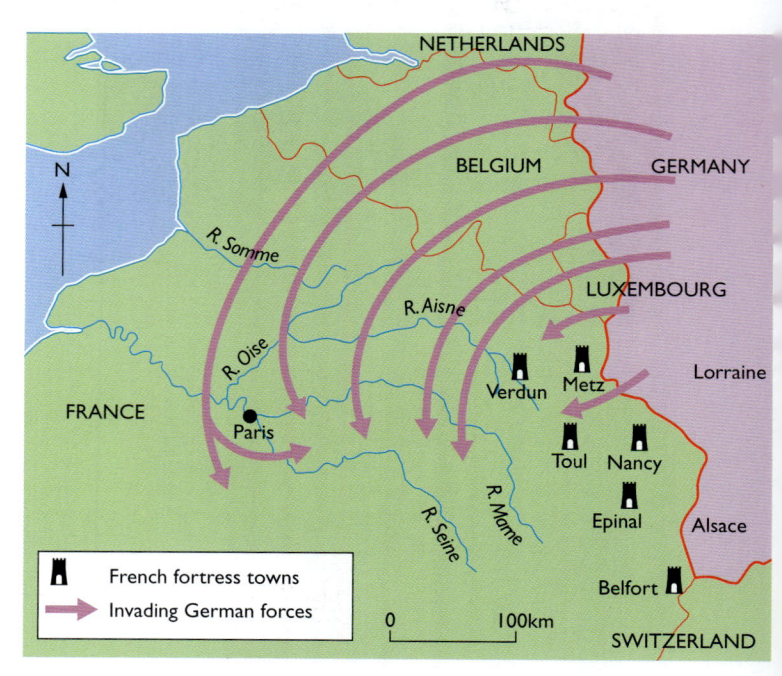

*Map showing the Schlieffen Plan, Germany's strategy for the invasion of France*

The War to End Wars 1914–1919

armies would quickly knock France out of the war and then deal with Russia.

How could they defeat the French in less than six weeks? The border with France was too well defended to attack – it was protected by strong French fortresses, as well as a great number of troops. Nevertheless, there was one gap in the French defences – the Belgian frontier. Belgium, however, was a **neutral** country whose neutrality was guaranteed by the Great Powers, including Britain. Despite this, von Schlieffen decided to attack through Belgium. The Belgian army was small and would easily be brushed aside. While the main French armies attacked through Alsace-Lorraine, the German armies would sweep through Belgium and into northern France. The French would realise their mistake too late, by which time Paris would have been taken and the French armies surrounded. With the fall of the French capital, all French enthusiasm for the war would collapse and their armies would surrender.

Schlieffen realised that the invasion of Belgium would force Britain into the war but believed that France would be defeated before the British armed forces could make any impact.

## What did it need to succeed?

The Schlieffen Plan made several assumptions.

- The Belgians would not resist, or if they did, they would be easily defeated and the German armies would quickly advance through the country.
- The French would attack through Alsace-Lorraine and would be too slow to realise their mistake and disrupt the German plan.
- Russia would take at least six weeks to mobilise and Germany would only need to send, at first, a small force to the east.
- The British Expeditionary Force would arrive too late to stop the German advance.

**Source A** British cartoon of early August 1914

PUNCH, OR THE LONDON CHARIVARI.—August 12, 1914.

NO THOROUGHFARE

BRAVO, BELGIUM!

### Tasks

1. What message is the cartoonist trying to get across in Source A?

2. Complete the flow diagram below to show the various stages of the Schlieffen Plan.

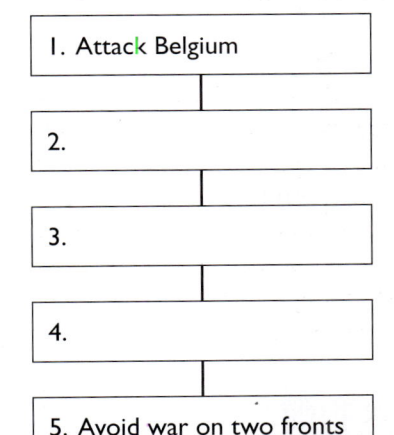

   1. Attack Belgium
   2. 
   3. 
   4. 
   5. Avoid war on two fronts

3. Look at what the plan needed to succeed. What do you think could go wrong?

The failure of the Schlieffen Plan

# Why did the Schlieffen Plan fail?

**The BEF**

The Kaiser had dismissed the BEF as a 'contemptible little army'. However the BEF, under the command of Sir John French, started to arrive in France on 18 August, much more quickly than the Germans had expected. It was a small but excellently trained force. The new German commander, von Moltke, had to transfer troops from the Eastern Front to face the BEF.

On 23 August the BEF stumbled into the Germans near the mining town of Mons. The BEF were heavily outnumbered and had to retreat. They had, however, further delayed the German advance. Three days later there was a further battle at Le Cateau. Again the British retreated but the Germans were slowed down.

**Source A** Photograph of Belgian troops guarding a bridge over a railway at Termonde, September 1914

**Source B** From a German soldier about the Battle of Mons

*From now on matters went from bad to worse. Wherever I looked, right or left, there were dead or wounded, quivering in convulsions, groaning terribly, blood oozing from flesh wounds. We had to go back. A bad defeat, there could be no denying it. In our first battle we had been badly beaten, and by the English – by the English we had so laughed at a few hours before.*

**Source C** An official British painting of 1914 of the charge of the British 9th Lancers at Mons, by Richard Caton Woodville II

Map showing the movements of the opposing armies in August 1914

The War to End Wars 1914–1919

**Changes to the plan**
Von Schlieffen did not live long enough to put his plan into action. In 1913 his dying words had been 'keep the right wing strong'. He urged that the right wing of the German army should be six times stronger than any other. The new German commander, von Moltke, ignored this advice and the army was not strong enough to carry out the plan. The German armies that invaded Belgium were 100,000 soldiers short because von Moltke sent additional forces to reinforce the Russian front.

Von Moltke made other crucial changes to the original plan. Schlieffen wanted a wide sweep through the Netherlands, Luxembourg and Belgium. This was changed to a narrower sweep attack through Belgium and Luxembourg. In addition, German armies were supposed to encircle Paris. This plan was abandoned in early September and they moved to the east, leading to the Battle of the Marne (see page 14).

**Belgian resistance**
The Belgians, using their forts, resisted and slowed down the German advance. On 3 August an army of over one million Germans marched into Belgium. Deep concrete forts protecting Antwerp, Liège and Namur delayed the Germans. Heavy guns had to be brought up to pound the defences to rubble. Antwerp did not surrender until October. Belgian resistance gave the British Expeditionary Force (BEF) time to arrive.

**German exhaustion**
The advance through Belgium and into northern France took its toll on the German soldiers.

**Source D** The diary entry of a German officer, September 1914

*Our soldiers stagger forward, their faces coated with dust, their uniforms in rags. They look like living scarecrows.*

**French resistance**
The French, as expected, had attacked Alsace-Lorraine and had suffered heavy casualties. The delays achieved by the Belgians and British gave the French time to move their troops towards Paris and make a stand on the Marne.

## Tasks

1. Source A is an official Belgian photograph. Devise a caption for the photograph that could have been used by the Belgian government.

2. What can you learn from Source B about the Battle of Mons? (This is an inference question. For further guidance see page 18.)

3. How useful is Source C as evidence of the Battle of Mons? (This is a utility question. For further guidance see pages 42 and 50.)

4. How important were each of the following countries in the failure of the Schlieffen Plan?

Make a copy of the table and give each country a rating with a brief explanation.

|  | Decisive | Important | Unimportant |
|---|---|---|---|
| Belgium |  |  |  |
| Britain |  |  |  |
| France |  |  |  |
| Germany |  |  |  |

5. Source D is the diary entry of a German officer for 2 September. Write possible entries in his diary for 3, 18 and 23 August.

The failure of the Schlieffen Plan

# Why was the Battle of the Marne, 5–19 September, decisive?

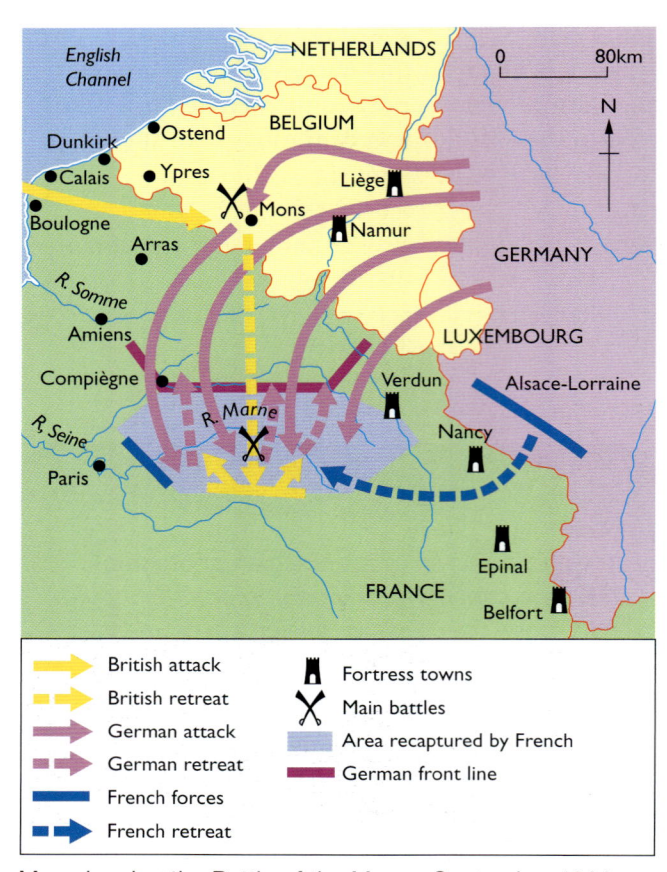

Map showing the Battle of the Marne, September 1914

A Paris taxi to take troops to the Marne

### Source A A French soldier remembers the Marne

*The wounded cry out. One of them begged the Colonel first to help him, then to finish him off. Finally the Colonel ordered an advance. 'Let's go boys, we must move forward. Your comrades are out there. You can't leave them alone.'*

By 5 September 1914 the German armies had reached the River Marne, just 65 km to the north-east of Paris. Many Parisians grabbed what belongings they could and fled the city. However, instead of moving to the west of Paris, as in the original plan, the German armies moved to the east. In addition, the two German armies that had advanced furthest, under Generals von Kluck and von Bulow, had split and a gap had appeared.

The French meanwhile had quickly moved their armies from Alsace-Lorraine northwards to the Marne to protect Paris. Their armies were further reinforced with every available soldier from Paris, transported by taxis and buses. Between the French armies and the Germans stood the BEF, pushed back from Belgium but still intact.

British **reconnaissance balloons** spotted the gap between the two German armies. Cautiously at first, the BEF advanced into the gap, supported by the French. Initially the Germans resisted and held their ground. The ensuing battle lasted for over a week across a front of 200 kilometres. Finally, the exhausted German armies fell back to a safe position 60 km north of the River Aisne.

The Battle of the Marne was the only decisive battle on the Western Front until 1918:

- It signalled the final failure of the Schlieffen Plan.
- The Germans reverted to Plan B, the race for the Channel ports.

### Tasks

1. What can you learn from Source A about the French troops at the Marne? (This is an inference question. For further guidance, see page 18.)

2. Imagine you are a military adviser to von Moltke in 1914 before the Battle of the Marne. What changes would you suggest to ensure that the Schlieffen Plan succeeds?

The War to End Wars 1914–1919

# Why was there a race for the sea?

Despite the retreat from the River Marne, the Germans were not defeated. Indeed they still occupied most of north-east France and Belgium.

They tried a new plan: to try to **outflank** the British and French armies by sweeping north. However, wherever they pushed, they found the French armies moving in the same direction.

The Germans also hoped to reach the English Channel and seize the ports. This would cut off the retreat of the BEF and prevent further British reinforcements. The BEF, however, also advanced north and there began a 'race to the sea'. The British arrived on the Belgian coast in time, helped by the Belgians who deliberately flooded their countryside, just as the Germans tried one last time to curve round northwards behind the Allies.

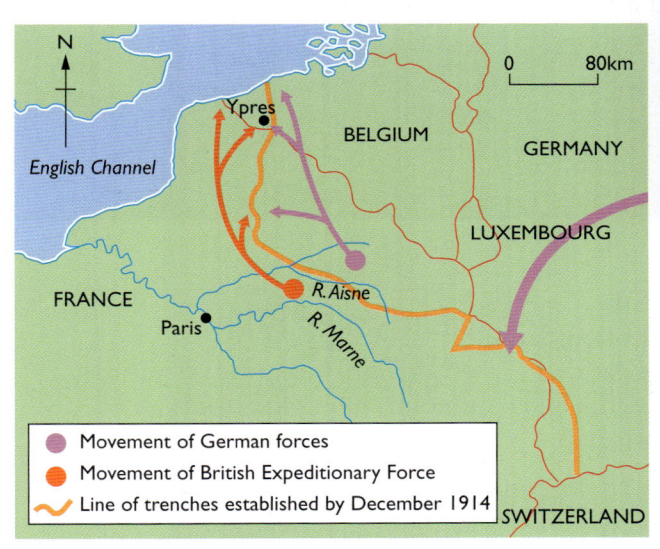

Map showing the 'race to the sea'

## The First Battle of Ypres, October 1914

When the British reached the sea, they sought to defend the Channel ports. In hastily dug trench positions they made their stand at the Belgian town of Ypres, which they nicknamed 'Wipers'. Here 13,000 of the best German soldiers attacked the British and were massacred. There was desperate hand-to-hand fighting in the woods that surrounded the town. The battle raged for a month.

As a result of the battle:

- the British suffered 50,000 casualties, including over 8,000 deaths, and the BEF was destroyed
- the Germans suffered 20,000 deaths
- the German advance was halted and the Channel ports saved.

**Source A** British troops arriving in the market place at Ypres, 13 October 1914

**Source B** A corporal in the BEF writing home after the First Battle of Ypres

*Of the 1,100 officers and men that came out to France at the start of the war, we have Major Yeadon and 80 men left. I believe you have plenty of soldiers at home. Well, we could do with a few here.*

### Tasks

1. What can you learn from Source B about the impact of the events of 1914 on the BEF? (This is an inference question. For further guidance see page 18.)

2. Describe what you can see in Source A. What changes to Ypres do you think would have taken place as a result of the battle?

The failure of the Schlieffen Plan

# What was the situation by the end of 1914?

A photograph of British troops in trenches in December 1914.

The war in France and Belgium was planned as 'a war of movement'. The rival armies would manoeuvre, trying to outflank their opponents. By Christmas 1914, however, it was clear that neither side was going to achieve a quick victory. The Schlieffen Plan and the German attempt to seize the Channel ports had failed.

Even so, the Germans showed no sign of giving in and were strong enough to resist any counter-attacks. The war on the Western Front had reached deadlock. No one could deliver the knockout blow. Both sides had lost well over half a million men in the summer and autumn battles. The losses had been so great that there was even talk of a negotiated peace. However, neither side was prepared to accept anything less than complete victory.

The armies of both sides began to dig in where they stood, and soon an elaborate network of trenches was constructed from the Channel coast to Switzerland (see map page 24). Trench warfare was supposed to last for the winter and then, in 1915, the war of movement would resume. In fact, the war in the trenches was to last for over three years.

## Christmas 1914

On Christmas Day, at various points along the front, an unofficial truce began and the shooting died away. German soldiers sang carols. British troops responded with their own. They then shouted greetings to each other. Even more surprisingly, in some places men from both sides climbed out of their trenches and walked into **no man's land**. There they swapped cigarettes and even played a game of football. Two days later, however, the shooting started again.

16  The War to End Wars 1914–1919

**Source A** German troops preparing their first trenches

**Source B** A letter from a British officer to *The Times* newspaper

*All this talk of hate, all this fury which has raged since the beginning of the war, was quelled and stayed by the magic of Christmas. Indeed one German in no man's land said 'But you are the same religion as us, and today is the Day of Peace!' It is a great hope for future peace when two great nations, hating each other as foes have seldom hated, should on Christmas Day lay down their arms, exchange smokes, and wish each other happiness.*

## Tasks

1. Source A shows German troops preparing their first trenches. Why were both sides able to prepare their trenches so quickly?

2. What can you learn from Source B about the unofficial Christmas Day truce? (This is an inference question. For further guidance, see page 18.)

3. Imagine you are a British journalist who witnessed the 'truce' of Christmas Day. Write the front page headlines and article describing what took place.

4. Using a diagram or illustration explain the difference between a war of movement and deadlock.

The failure of the Schlieffen Plan

# Examination practice

> **Source A** From the memoirs of David Lloyd George, the British Chancellor of the Exchequer in 1914
>
> *When I first heard of the assassination of Franz Ferdinand I felt it was a grave matter. However, soon my fears were calmed as the Kaiser left on a yachting holiday. However, an important Hungarian lady called on me and told me that we were taking the murder of the heir to the Austrian throne too lightly. It had provoked a storm in Austria and might lead to war with Serbia.*

> **Source B** An official history of the First World War describes the First Battle of Ypres
>
> *On the 13 November the Germans sent 13,000 of their best soldiers to force a way through the British defences. They came on at a steady pace and despite their casualties they penetrated the British line at several points. A British counter-attack followed which cleared the woods. There was deadly hand-to-hand combat after which most of the German troops lay dead or wounded.*

## Question 1 – Inference

What can you learn from Source A about reactions to the assassination of Franz Ferdinand?

(4 marks)

### How to answer

This is an inference question. You are being asked to give the message or messages of the source, to read between the lines of what is written. For example in Source A there are at least two 'messages':

> **Source A**
>
> When I first heard of the assassination of Franz Ferdinand I felt it was a grave matter. However, soon *my fears were calmed as the Kaiser left on a yachting holiday*. However, an important Hungarian lady called on me and told me that we were taking the murder of the heir to the Austrian throne too lightly. *It had provoked a storm in Austria* and might lead to war with Serbia.

*The message could be that Britain and Germany did not believe it was a serious event.*

*The message could be that it had serious repercussions in Austria.*

## Question 2 – Inference

What can you learn from Source B about the First Battle of Ypres?

(4 marks)

### Now have a go yourself

- Begin your answer with 'This source suggests ...' This should help you get a message or messages from the source.
- Avoid repeating the content.
- Look for key words in the source that might lead to inferences.
- You could tackle this by copying the source and highlighting different messages in different colours to help you identify the important points, as in the example given for question 1.

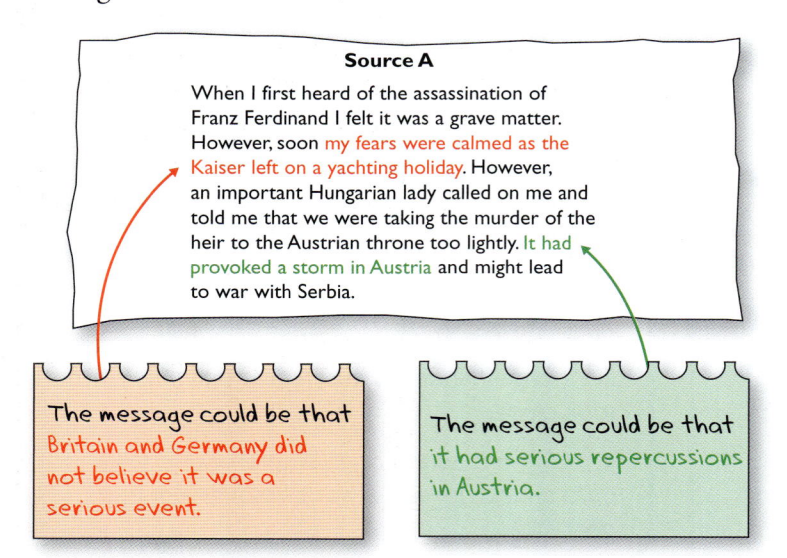

The overall message could be that the Great Powers, with the exception of Austria, under-estimated the importance of the assassination.

# 2 Stalemate on the Western Front, 1915–17

**Source A** British advertising poster of 1915

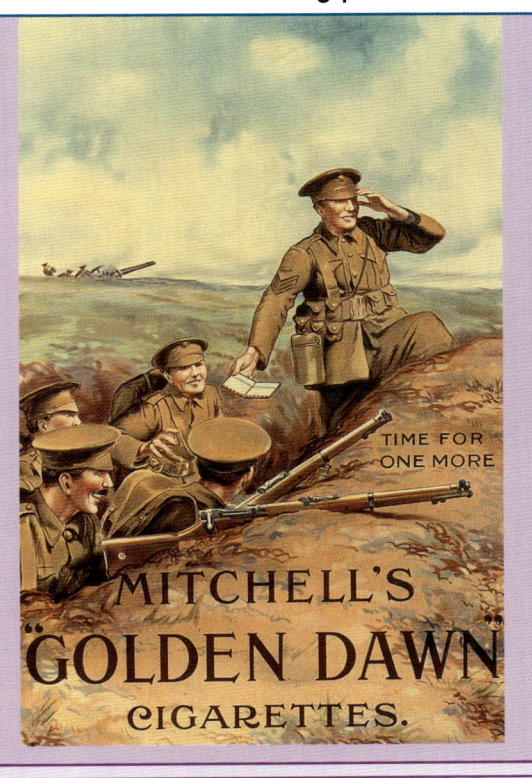

**Source B** A young German soldier describes going over the top on the Western Front

*At noon we went over the top. After less than a hundred yards we ran up against almost a concrete wall of machine-gun bullets. My company commander had his face shot away. Another man yelling and whimpering held his hand to his belly and through his fingers, his stomach protruded. A young boy cried for his mother, bright red blood spurting out from his face.*

## Tasks

1. What message is the poster trying to get across in Source A?

2. What can you learn from Source B about trench warfare? (Remember how to answer this type of question? For further guidance see page 18.)

3. What differences are there between Sources A and B in their view of trench warfare?

Both sides dug what they believed would be temporary trenches for the winter of 1914–15, fully expecting to break through and resume a war of movement in 1915. No such breakthrough was achieved, and there was deadlock on the Western Front for the next three years. As the trench systems became stronger and more complex, it became even more difficult to gain ground. Both sides attempted to end the stalemate: the Germans made a prolonged attack at Verdun in 1916; the British launched major offensives on the Somme in 1916 and at Passchendaele in 1917. All failed and led to very heavy casualties.

This chapter answers the following questions:

- What was the trench system?
- What was it like for the soldiers in the trenches?
- Why was there a stalemate for three years?
- What part did Haig play in the stalemate?
- Why was there no breakthrough at the Somme and at Passchendaele?

### Source skills

You will be given practice in the second type of source question in Paper 2, which asks you to cross-reference three sources. It is worth six marks.

# What was the trench system?

Although initially each side dug one line of the trenches, during the course of the next three years the trench systems became stronger and more sophisticated. Eventually there were as many as four lines of trenches in some places, with **dug-outs** ten metres below ground level.

**Source A** The crew of a German machine gun on the Western Front

Behind the front line were the support or **reserve trenches** in case the front line should be captured. They were also a resting place for the front-line troops. In some places there were even third and fourth lines of trenches. Running between these lines were **communication trenches**, which were used to move troops and supplies. Everything going up to the front had to use these trenches – fresh troops, water, food, supplies and mail.

**No man's land** was a desolate area between the two rival trench systems, which could be as little as one hundred metres wide. **Artillery** shells had destroyed any drainage ditches, creating a sea of mud and shell craters in which many soldiers drowned.

## Tasks

1. Why was the machine gun in Source A an ideal weapon for defending the trench system?

2. Very few soldiers who went over the top were able to reach the enemy trenches. Working in pairs, use the information and diagrams on these two pages to make a list of the obstacles they would have to overcome.

No man's land at Ypres, October 1917

The War to End Wars 1914–1919

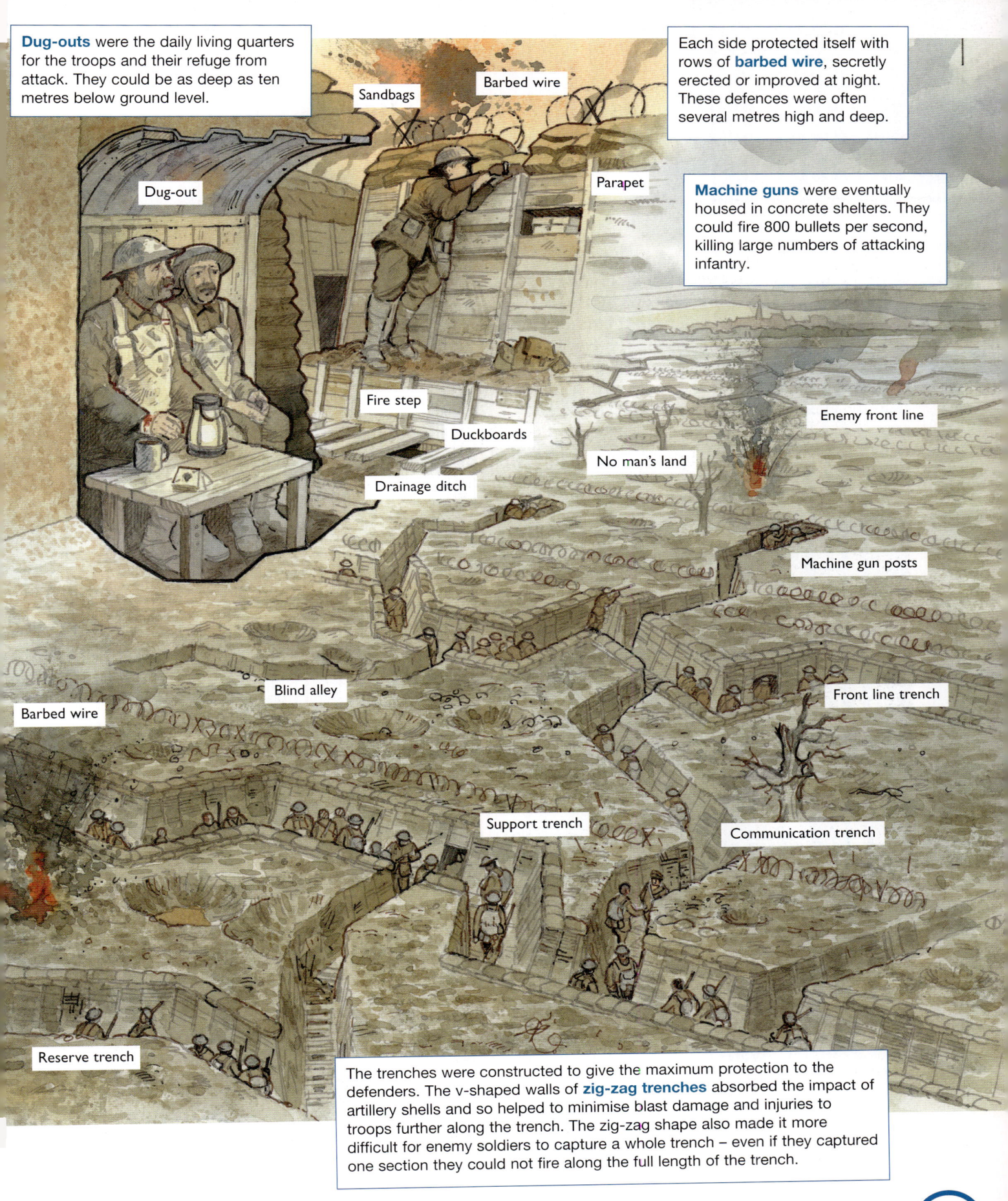

**Dug-outs** were the daily living quarters for the troops and their refuge from attack. They could be as deep as ten metres below ground level.

Each side protected itself with rows of **barbed wire**, secretly erected or improved at night. These defences were often several metres high and deep.

**Machine guns** were eventually housed in concrete shelters. They could fire 800 bullets per second, killing large numbers of attacking infantry.

Sandbags
Barbed wire
Parapet
Dug-out
Fire step
Duckboards
No man's land
Enemy front line
Drainage ditch
Machine gun posts
Blind alley
Front line trench
Barbed wire
Support trench
Communication trench
Reserve trench

The trenches were constructed to give the maximum protection to the defenders. The v-shaped walls of **zig-zag trenches** absorbed the impact of artillery shells and so helped to minimise blast damage and injuries to troops further along the trench. The zig-zag shape also made it more difficult for enemy soldiers to capture a whole trench – even if they captured one section they could not fire along the full length of the trench.

Stalemate on the Western Front, 1915–17

# What was it like for the soldiers in the trenches?

Soldiers not only fought but also lived in the trenches. Most days were very monotonous and boring and seemed to pass very slowly. People were killed, but there were few great battles. Men sat around reading or smoking or playing chess. Some wrote letters home. These were checked by a **censor** before being posted. Anything that might help the enemy or reduce morale on the home front was crossed out with a blue pencil.

**Source A** Men of the Border Regiment resting in dug-outs in 1916

**Source B** George Coppard remembers the food rations

*Wrapping loose rations such as tea, cheese and meat was not considered necessary. They were all tipped into a sandbag, a ghastly mix-up resulting. In wet weather their condition was unbelievable. Maconochie, a 'dinner in a tin', was my favourite. I could polish off one very quickly, but the usual share-out was one tin for four men.*

**Source C** Australian troops preparing food, 1916

## Food

Troops did not often go hungry although there was little variety in their diet. They often ate 'bully' or corned beef with ten men sharing a loaf of bread. In an emergency there were always hard biscuits, but these were like concrete.

Cooking facilities were very basic. Some troops had no hot meals for weeks on end. Generally the food was prepared in the same few pots, making it all taste the same. Water was generally brought in petrol cans to the front, where chloride of lime was added to kill the germs. This made it taste awful. In winter the men even melted snow and ice to make tea.

## Hygiene

Diseases were common in the trenches where men crowded together in unhygienic conditions. Everyone had lice – in his hair, on his body and in every part of his clothing. Men were occasionally deloused but the lice would reappear within a few days.

There were rats everywhere too, feeding on rotting bodies and horse carcasses. They even nibbled the troops as they slept.

Much more serious were the epidemics. Germs in food and water led to **typhoid**, **cholera** and **dysentery**.

The War to End Wars 1914–1919

> **Source D** A British soldier describes rats in the trenches
>
> *Whilst asleep during the night, we were frequently awakened by rats running over us. When this happened too often for my liking, I would lie on my back and wait for a rat to linger on my legs, then violently heave my legs upward, throwing the rat in the air. Occasionally I would hear a grunt when the rat landed on a fellow victim.*

## Weather

The soldiers also had to put up with extremes of weather – snow and frost in the winter and rain at any time of year made conditions in the trenches miserable. It was not unusual to find half a metre of water in the bottom of the trenches. Soldiers who had to stand in water for long periods developed a condition called trench foot, which in the worst cases led to them needing to have their feet amputated.

> **Source E** Sergeant Harry Roberts, who lived in a flooded trench for six days, describes the effects of trench foot
>
> *Your feet swell to two or three times their normal size and go completely dead. You could stick a bayonet into them and not feel a thing. If you are lucky enough not to lose your feet and the swelling begins to go down, it is then that the indescribable agony begins. I have heard men cry with the pain and many had to have their feet and legs amputated.*

## Dangers

There were many dangers besides the obvious risk of being killed in a battle.

- Enemy marksmen known as snipers waited for an unwary soldier to pop his head above the parapet. Many unsuspecting new arrivals were killed this way.
- Enemy bombardment, which happened most days, could lead to injury or death from flying splinters and debris.
- Poisonous gas, first used by the Germans in April 1915 (see page 44), caused death and a range of injuries.

Some soldiers suffered from shell shock as a result of the constant strain of living under shellfire. Early on in the war the army did not understand that shell shock was a form of mental illness, and many men, unable to fight, were shot as cowards.

> **Source F** A soldier describes shell shock
>
> *His steel hat was at the back of his head and his mouth slobbered, and two comrades could not hold him still. These badly shell-shocked boys clawed their mouths ceaselessly. Others sat in the field hospitals in a state of coma, dazed as though deaf, and actually dumb.*

### Tasks

**1.** How useful are Sources A and B as evidence of life in the trenches? (This is a utility question. For further guidance see pages 42 and 50.)

**2.** Letters from the front were censored. Rewrite the following letter, removing the parts you think would be censored. Explain why you have removed them.

> Dear Mam,
> At the moment I am in a trench near to Ypres. I have made some really good friends and enjoy the comradeship but the food is awful and yesterday someone in my trench was shot by a sniper. We spend most of the day playing cards and smoking because it is so boring. There are rats everywhere and yesterday I had to be deloused.
> Give my love to all the family.

**3.** 'The food was the worst part of life in the trenches.' Use Sources A–F, and your own knowledge, to explain whether you agree with this view. (This is a synthesis question. For further guidance see pages 74–76.)

# Why was there a stalemate for three years?

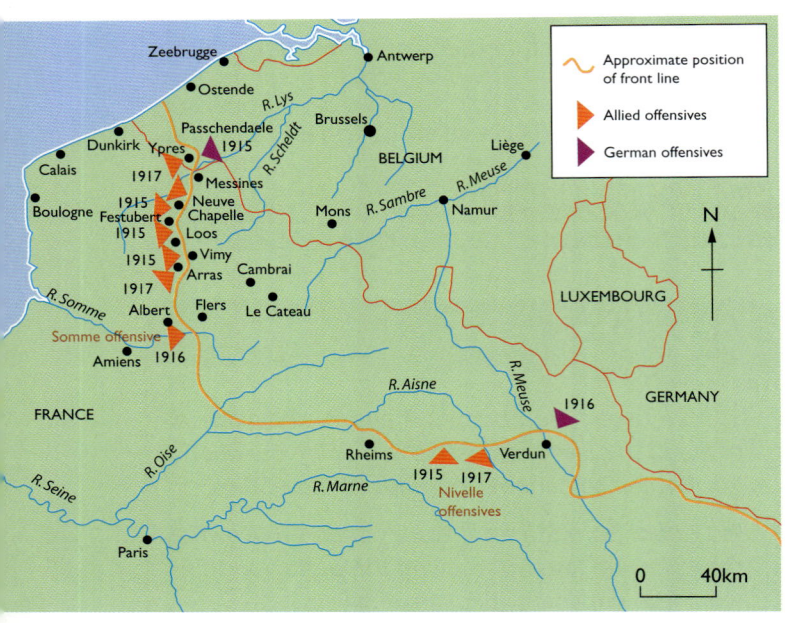

A map showing the main **offensives** on the Western Front, 1915–17

Both sides made attempts to break through between 1915 and 1917, without success. There were several reasons for the stalemate.

## The trench system
In the First World War infantrymen were supposed to attack quickly through gaps in the enemy trenches. This proved impossible against trenches that were defended by barbed wire and sandbags. Mud made **cavalry** charges ineffective.

## The machine gun
Machine guns were ideal defensive weapons. They could fire up to 600 rounds a minute and were able to cut down lines of attackers, causing huge casualties. The German Maxim gun accounted for 90 per cent of Allied victims in the Battle of the Somme (see pages 26–27).

## The failure of new weapons
Several new weapons were developed but none was successful in helping to achieve a breakthrough.

- The invention of the gas mask reduced the effectiveness of poisonous gas.
- The early tanks were slow and cumbersome, and many broke down. They were not used effectively until 1918.
- Heavy guns could cause considerable damage to enemy trenches but could not destroy the barbed wire or achieve a breakthrough. If anything, they made the task of the attacking side even more difficult, since no man's land became badly churned up by the bombardment, thus slowing the advancing troops.
- The flame-thrower was unreliable and quite likely to explode and kill the soldier using it.

## The commanders
Trench warfare was a new kind of fighting. No one really knew how to win a war like this. So the generals fell back on the ideas they had used successfully in past wars, such as mass cavalry or infantry attacks. The French commander, Marshal Joffre, believed that the 'spirit' of the French soldiers would see them across no man's land. The commanders on both sides persisted for three years with the belief that using large numbers of troops in an attack would achieve a breakthrough against machine guns and barbed wire.

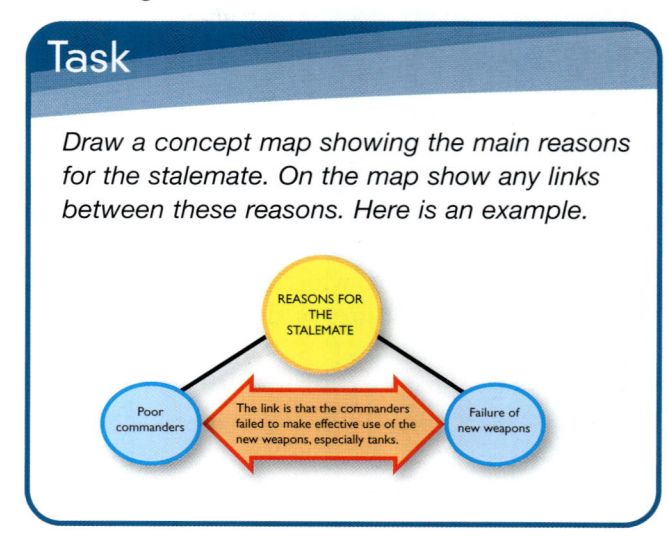

### Task
Draw a concept map showing the main reasons for the stalemate. On the map show any links between these reasons. Here is an example.

REASONS FOR THE STALEMATE — Poor commanders — Failure of new weapons. The link is that the commanders failed to make effective use of the new weapons, especially tanks.

The War to End Wars 1914–1919

# What part did Haig play in the stalemate?

Sir Douglas Haig was appointed commander of the British forces on the Western Front in December 1915. He has come in for much criticism. He was nicknamed the 'butcher of the Somme' because of the heavy casualties during the Somme **offensive** (see pages 26–27). He was blamed for his failure to break the stalemate.

## Evidence for the 'Butcher'

Haig believed in a policy of attrition, which meant wearing the enemy down with constant attacks even if it meant heavy casualties.

### Source A Haig writing in 1919

In the course of the struggle, losses are bound to be heavy on both sides, for in this the price of victory is paid. There is no way of avoiding this although our total losses in the war may have been greater than were to be expected.

### Source B A letter written to the *Daily Telegraph* in November 1916

We are slowly but surely killing off the best of the male population of these islands. Can we afford to go on paying the same sort of price for the same sort of gain?

### Source C From a school textbook about the First World War, 1998

The High Command, and especially Haig, could not think of any other form of warfare except to throw into battle large numbers of men, month after month. Haig's method of winning the war was clumsy, expensive in loss of life and based on a misreading of the facts.

## Evidence against the 'Butcher'

Haig faced a difficult task. Trench warfare was a new kind of fighting.

### Source D Haig writing in 1919

We attacked whenever possible, because a defensive policy involves the loss of the initiative. The object of all war is victory and a defensive attitude can never bring this about.

### Source E A historian writing in 1991

If the criterion of a successful general is to win wars, Haig must be judged a success. The cost of the victory was appalling, but Haig's military methods were in line with the ideas of the time, when attrition was the method all sides used to achieve victory.

### Source F From a modern world history textbook, written in 2001

Haig believed that the key objectives of his offensives were achieved. The Battle of the Somme saved Verdun and the French army. Passchendaele took the pressure off a French army close to breaking point. Some of Germany's best troops were killed in both 1916 and 1917, preparing the way for the Allied successes of 1918.

## Tasks

1. Does Source D support the evidence of Source C about Haig? Explain your answer.
(This is a cross-referencing question. For further guidance see pages 30–31.)

2. Using the evidence from Sources D, E and F write a reply to Source B, which defends Haig.

3. Which of the following statements do you most agree with?
- Haig deserves the title of the 'Butcher of the Somme'.
- Haig does not deserve the title of the 'Butcher of the Somme'.
- Haig's methods did result in heavy casualties but did bring some success.

Write a paragraph justifying your choice, using evidence from the sources.

Stalemate on the Western Front, 1915–17

# Why was there no breakthrough at the Somme and at Passchendaele?

The British launched two major offensives, on the Somme in 1916 and at Passchendaele in 1917, but neither achieved a breakthrough.

## The Somme, July–November 1916

The Somme offensive was launched for several reasons:

- Haig believed in a policy of attrition or wearing down the Germans by constantly attacking.
- The British Secretary of State for War, Lord Kitchener, had launched a major recruitment campaign in 1915. As a result, the British army had been strengthened by about one million new recruits. In addition, the British were reinforced by troops from parts of the British empire, including Australia, India, New Zealand, Canada and the Caribbean.
- The Germans had attacked the French fortress system at Verdun in February, and the French were desperate for help. They suggested a joint Anglo-French offensive to take the pressure off Verdun.
- The Somme was chosen as it was the area of the front where the French and British armies met. However, it was also the area in which the German defences were strongest.

## 1 July 1916

The offensive was preceded by a week-long bombardment, with 1500 guns shelling the German lines continuously. The **barrage** did not destroy the barbed wire and served only to warn the Germans that an attack was imminent. They further strengthened their defences. When the shelling ended, the Germans, who had been sheltering in deep dug-outs, quickly took up their posts at the machine guns.

The first British soldiers went over the top at 7.30a.m. They had been told to form 'waves' and walk slowly across no man's land as there would be no German survivors of the bombardment. In fact they walked into the worst slaughter ever suffered by the British army – nearly 20,000 killed and 40,000 wounded on the first day.

> **Source B** Sergeant Cook describes what happened
>
> *The first Rifle Brigade advanced in perfect order. Everything was working smoothly. The first line had nearly reached the German front line, when all at once machine-gun opened up all along our front with a murderous fire. We were caught in the open, with no shelter. Men were falling like ninepins.*

## July to November 1916

Despite the losses, Haig, under pressure from the French, continued the offensive. In September tanks were used for the first time (see page 47) but were ineffective. The villages of Beaumont Hamel and Beaucourt were captured using a new tactic, the creeping barrage, whereby the infantry attacked at the same time as the artillery bombarded the German positions. Bad weather finally brought an end to the battle in November.

> **Source A** Haig writing after the battle
>
> *The German defences consisted of several lines of trenches, well-provided with bomb-proof shelters and protected by wire entanglements forty yards wide, built of iron stakes interlaced with barbed wire. The woods and the villages between the trenches had been turned into veritable fortresses.*

> **Source C** Haig's views after the battle
>
> *By the third week in November the three main objectives with which we commenced had already been achieved. Verdun had been relieved, the German forces had been held on the Western Front and the enemy's strength had been considerably worn down.*

The War to End Wars 1914–1919

**Source D** A still from *The Battle of the Somme, 1916*, an official film made by the British government to be shown to the public, showing attacks by British troops

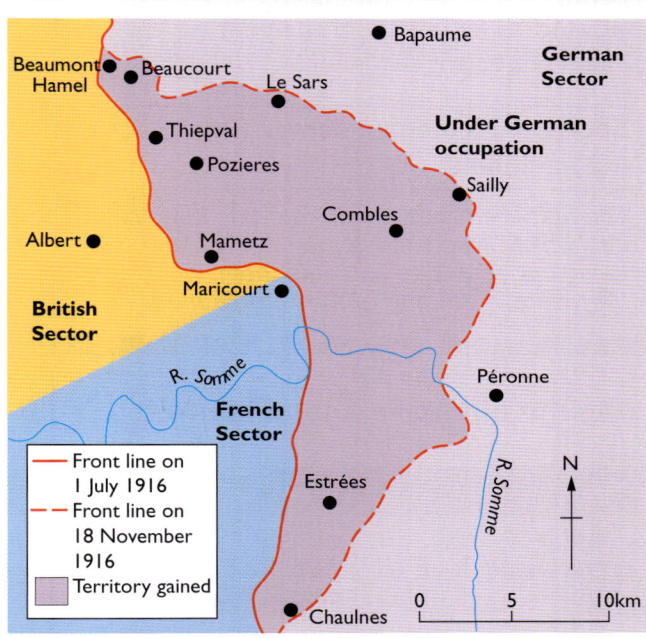

**Source F** An official German photograph of a British soldier killed on the Somme

A map showing territory gained in the Battle of the Somme, July–November 1916

## What did it achieve?

By the time the battle ended, the Germans had been pushed back a little but there had been no breakthrough. The British and imperial forces had over 400,000 casualties.

**Source E** From an official history of the war

*For this disastrous loss of the finest men there was only a small gain of ground to show. Never again was the spirit or the quality of the officers and men so high. The losses were heavy and could not be replaced.*

### Tasks

1. How useful are Sources D and F as evidence about the Battle of the Somme? (This is a utility question. For further guidance, see pages 42 and 50.)

2. 'The Battle of the Somme was a total failure.' Use Sources A–F and your own knowledge to explain whether you agree with this view. (This is a synthesis question. For further guidance, see pages 74–76.)

Stalemate on the Western Front, 1915–17

## Passchendaele, July–November 1917

The other major British attempt to achieve a breakthrough was the Third Battle of Ypres or Passchendaele.

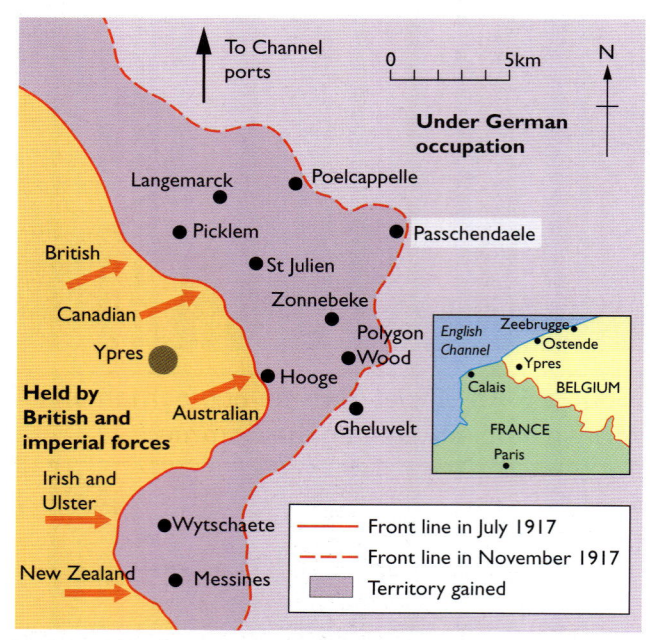

Map showing the Third Battle of Ypres

### Why was the offensive launched?

Haig had three main reasons for launching the offensive:

- Once again he needed to take the pressure off the French and prevent their military collapse. Some of the French troops had **mutinied** in April and May 1917.
- He still believed in attrition. He was convinced that the Germans had been greatly weakened by the offensives of 1916 and were on the verge of collapse.
- He was convinced that he could achieve a quick breakthrough at Ypres. The British could then advance north and capture the Belgian ports of Zeebrugge and Ostende, which were being used by the Germans as **U-boat** bases.

### 'The Battle of the Mud'

The first attack took place on 31 July 1917. There was no breakthrough and, within a week, the British had lost 30,000 men. By October the fighting had reached the village of Passchendaele, about 11 kilometres from the starting point. On 6 November Canadian troops finally captured the village and then, because it was so late in the year and the conditions on the battlefield were getting worse, the offensive was called off. There was no breakthrough because:

- during the attacks the Germans used a deadly gas, mustard gas, for the first time, which totally confused the British troops (see page 44). Gas masks provided no protection from this nerve gas.
- it rained throughout August. The whole battlefield soon turned into a sea of mud, making it impossible for tanks, horses or guns to advance. The impact of the poor weather was the main reason for the failure of the offensive.

> **Source A** Lieutenant James Dale describes the battlefield
>
> *The battlefield was turned into one huge quagmire, into which were sucked men, horses and guns, it being impossible to extricate them, when once they were in the grip of this terrible mud.*

### Was the offensive a total failure?

| Yes | No |
| --- | --- |
| There was no breakthrough. | The pressure was taken off the French, who recovered. |
| Britain and its empire lost 250,000 men and the Germans only 200,000. Attrition was not working. | Germans suffered over 200,000 casualties during the Third Battle of Ypres. |
| The British had gained only 11 kilometres of mud. | The Germans were seriously weakened, which contributed to their eventual defeat the following year. |

The War to End Wars 1914–1919

**Source B** Canadian troops in the mud at Passchendaele

## Tasks

**1.** Does Source B support the evidence of Source A about the battlefield at Passchendaele? Explain your answer. (This is a cross-referencing question. For further guidance, see pages 30–31.)

**2.** Which of the following interpretations best describe the Third Battle of Ypres?

- It was a total failure and achieved nothing.
- It achieved its main objectives.
- It was mainly a failure.

Give a reason for your choice.

## The situation by the end of 1917

After three years of trench warfare, neither side had achieved a breakthrough and had suffered very heavy casualties. For example, the British had lost 250,000 during the Third Battle of Ypres. For the Germans, however, the situation was more serious. Not only were the German people running short of food, but the USA had entered the war on the Allied side. When US troops arrived on the Western Front a German victory would be almost impossible.

Stalemate on the Western Front, 1915–17

# Examination practice

**Source A** Report from Sir Douglas Haig on the first day of the Somme

*Yes, we had some casualties. Overall, however, a very successful attack this morning. All went like clockwork. The battle is going well for us and already the Germans are surrendering freely. The enemy is so short of men that he is collecting them from all parts of the line. Our troops are in wonderful spirits and full of confidence.*

**Source C** From the diary of a British soldier, 1 July 1916

*It was a bloody disaster. As soon as the signal was given machine-gun fire opened up on us. The heaviest casualties occurred on passing through the gaps in our own wire where the men were mown down in heaps. There were dead and wounded everywhere.*

**Source B** A photograph of wounded British troops, 1 July 1916

## Question 1 – cross-referencing

Does Source C support the evidence of Sources A and B about the first day of the Somme? Explain your answer.

(6 marks)

### How to answer

Use the planning grid on this page to help you organise your answer and the flow chart opposite to show you how to construct your answer.

## Planning grid

| Sources | Details that support each other | Details that differ | Extent of support |
|---|---|---|---|
| C/A | Both mention casualties | C – disaster and A – success | Very little support |
| C/B | | | |

- Examine Sources C and A. Make a note of any parts of Sources C and A that support each other. There may be no support.
- Now explain any areas of support between the two sources.

> Example:
> Source C supports Source A because both sources suggest there were casualties.

- Make a note of any parts of Sources C and A that differ from each other. There may be no differences.
- Now explain any differences between the two sources.

> Example:
> Source C suggests that the attack was a total failure with many dead and wounded. Source A, on the other hand, believes it was a success with many Germans surrendering.

- Now make a judgement on how much C supports A. Use the judgement line below to help you.
  
  **Strongly support   Some support   Very little support   No support**
- Use judgement words or phrases such as 'there is strong support'/ 'there is little support' or 'strongly agree'/ 'very little agreement'.

> Example:
> For the most part Source C strongly disagrees with Source A as they have almost opposite views on the outcome of the first day of the Somme.

Now do the same with Sources C and B.
- Examine Sources C and B. Make a note of any parts of Sources C and B that support each other. There may be no support.
- Now explain any areas of support between the two sources.

> Example:
> Source C supports Source B as Source C suggests there were heavy casualties with many dead and wounded. Source B shows a number of British wounded after the first day of the Somme.

- Make a note of any parts of Sources C and B that differ from each other. There may be no differences.
- Now explain any differences between the two sources.

> Example:
> Source C does not fully support the evidence of Source B. Source C suggests that there were many casualties with a great number of soldiers killed. The full scale of the casualties is not shown in Source B.

- Now make a judgement on how much C supports B. Use the judgement line below to help you.
  
  **Strongly support   Some support   Very little support   No support**
- Use judgement words or phrases such as 'there is strong support'/ 'there is little support' or 'strongly agree'/ 'very little agreement'.

> Example:
> Source C strongly supports the evidence of Source B as both sources suggest there were heavy casualties and that the first day was a disaster.

Finally, write a conclusion.
- Begin with the word 'overall'.
- Make a judgement on how much support there is between C and each of the other two sources. Remember to use judgement words/phrases.

> Example:
> Overall Source C strongly supports the evidence of Source B, especially about the casualties on the first day of the Somme. On the other hand it strongly disagrees with Source A, which suggests that the first day was a success.

## Question 2 — cross-referencing

Does Source C support the evidence of Sources A and B about the conditions on the Western Front? Explain your answer.

(6 marks)

**Source A** From a school textbook on the First World War, describing the conditions at Passchendaele

The ground here was flat, and soggy from recent rain. The whole battlefield had turned into a sea of mud, making it impossible for tanks, guns or supplies to advance. Horses and men were trapped and died in the shell holes created by the heavy bombardment. Even the soldiers could hardly move through the porridge-like slime which often reached up to their knees.

**Source C** Description of the battle area by a German soldier, February 1915

You can't possibly picture to yourself what such a battlefield looks like. It is impossible to describe it. Every foot of ground churned up a yard deep by the heaviest shells. Dead animals, houses and churches so utterly destroyed by shell fire that they can never be of any use again.

**Source B** Painting of the trench area by C. R. W. Nevison, drawn after the First World War

### Now have a go yourself
- Make a copy of the table below and plan your answer.

| Sources | Details that support each other | Details that differ | Extent of support |
|---|---|---|---|
| C/A | | | |
| C/B | | | |

- Write up your answer following the steps explained on page 31.

# 3 The war at sea and Gallipoli

> **Source A** An official German statement, June 1916
>
> The Kaiser addresses the crews of the High Seas Fleet. 'The British fleet was beaten at Jutland. The first great hammer blow was struck, and the halo of British world naval supremacy has disappeared for ever.'

> **Source B** From a textbook about the First World War, 1998
>
> The Kaiser insisted on regarding the battle as a victory. He was quite wrong. Jellicoe had not won a great victory but he had not suffered a defeat. The Kaiser was warned that the High Seas Fleet needed a month to make good the damage it suffered. It never emerged from port again.

> **Task**
>
> Does Source B support the evidence of Source A in its views of the Battle of Jutland? Explain your answer. (Remember how to answer this type of question? For further guidance see pages 30–31.)

The German **fleet** posed several threats to the British during the First World War. Early on in the war German cruisers raided the British east coast. In 1916 the combined fleets of both countries fought a major sea battle, off the Jutland peninsula in the North Sea. The results of the battle were unique as both sides claimed victory. However, it was the British **blockade** of Germany that had the most decisive impact on the eventual outcome of the war. As well as the war at sea this chapter examines the Gallipoli campaign, an ambitious **amphibious operation** to try to break the stalemate on the Western Front. It was a disastrous failure.

This chapter answers the following questions:

- How did the German navy threaten Britain?
- What were the key events in the North Sea, 1914–15?
- What was the importance of the Battle of Jutland?
- Why did the Allies launch the Gallipoli campaign?
- Why did the Gallipoli campaign fail?

## Source skills
This chapter gives you guidance on the third source question on Paper 2. This is the utility question, which asks you to decide how useful two sources are. It is worth eight marks.

# How did the German navy threaten Britain?

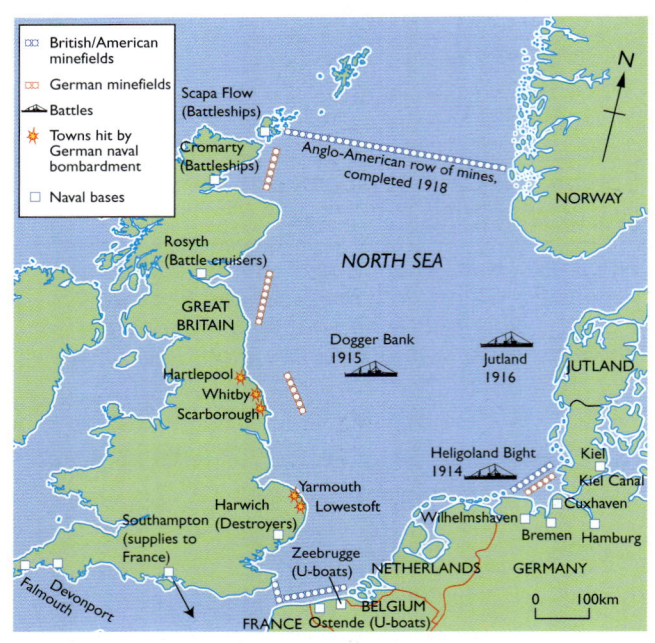

Map showing the main events in the North Sea, 1914–18

Control of the sea was important to both sides. The German navy threatened Britain in several ways:

- The British Isles were dependent on ships bringing in food, raw materials and other goods from abroad.
- Britain needed to be able to send reinforcements and fresh supplies across the Channel to the Western Front.
- Britain had a worldwide empire. Its only means of communication was by sea.

The British navy threatened Germany because:

- the British could blockade the German ports and cut off its overseas trade.
- Germany had an empire in Africa and the Far East. Like Britain, its only link with its overseas territories was by sea.

| British navy | German navy |
| --- | --- |
| The British had the largest fleet, with 29 dreadnoughts. These were anchored at Scapa Flow, a protected and sheltered bay in the Orkney islands, and at Cromarty. The battle cruisers were at Rosyth. | The German fleet was smaller, with only seventeen dreadnoughts in 1914. The German High Seas fleet spent most of the time at its base in Wilhelmshaven. |
| The British also had a long naval tradition, having controlled the seas throughout the nineteenth century. | Germany had no naval tradition. The Kaiser had built up the navy in the preceding fourteen years. |
| Britain had one more advantage. Early in the war a German cruiser, *Magdeburg,* was sunk by Russian ships in the Baltic Sea. The body of a German officer was found clutching the German naval code book. From then on Britain was able to decode German messages and knew when enemy ships were leaving port. | Germany did have several advantages over Britain:<br><br>- The German ships were of superior design, especially in the quality of their steel armour protection.<br>- The German gunners proved themselves to be superior marksmen.<br>- Most German shells, unlike their British counterparts, exploded on hitting enemy ships. |

## Task

*Examine the advantages and disadvantages of each side in the war at sea. Which country would be favourite to win the war in the North Sea? Give reasons for your answer.*

# What were the key events in the North Sea, 1914–15?

One of the first things Britain did on the outbreak of war was to order a naval blockade of Germany. This meant stopping all ships heading for German ports and turning back or sinking any found to be carrying food or supplies such as oil, steel or chemicals. During the course of the war about 12,000 ships were intercepted while fewer than 80 slipped through. By 1916 there were serious food shortages, which led to riots in a number of German towns. Some Germans called the winter of 1916 the 'turnip winter' because turnips seemed to be the only food that people could get to eat.

## The Battle of Heligoland Bight

This was the first naval battle of the First World War, and it took place in August 1914. Fast British **destroyers** deliberately sailed close to the German coast. They were pursued by more powerful German cruisers, which sailed into a trap – the British battle cruiser fleet under Admiral Beatty was waiting for them further out at sea. Three German cruisers and a destroyer were sunk. This gave great encouragement to the British public at this very early stage of the war, and Admiral Beatty became a popular hero.

## German raids on the east coast

In December 1914 the Germans decided to raid the east coast of England. This would (a) strike a blow at the morale of the British people and the reputation of the British navy and (b) force the navy to spread out its fleet along Britain's North Sea coast. This, in turn, would allow the German fleet to target single British ships without having to face the full 'Grand Fleet'.

The first raid was on Hartlepool at 8.10a.m. on 16 December. Whitby and Scarborough were also shelled that day and about 500 civilians were killed or wounded. The British public was outraged and, at first, criticised its own navy for failing to protect its coastline. One British headline said 'Germans creep out to attack east coast'.

**REMEMBER SCARBOROUGH!** The Germans who brag of their "CULTURE" have shown what it is made of by murdering defenceless women and children at SCARBOROUGH. But this only strengthens **GREAT BRITAIN'S** resolve to crush the **GERMAN BARBARIANS** **ENLIST NOW!**

Poster issued by the British government soon after the attack on Scarborough

## The Battle of Dogger Bank

On 24 January 1915 the British intercepted German radio signals suggesting the German battle cruiser fleet was sailing to Dogger Bank to attack the British fishing fleet. Admiral Beatty's battle cruisers lay in wait and, in the ensuing battle, two German battle cruisers were sunk. The German fleet had been taken by surprise and there were no further raids on the British coast. But the battle was not a total success for the British. Beatty's flagship, HMS *Lion*, was damaged and had to slow down, enabling remaining German ships to escape.

### Tasks

**1.** Look at the poster above and devise an alternative German poster about the raids on Britain.

**2.** Draw a table showing British and German successes in two different columns for the events of 1914–16.

**3.** Overall, which country was more successful in the North Sea in the first two years of the war? Explain your answer.

The war at sea and Gallipoli

# What was the importance of the Battle of Jutland?

The most important battle in the war at sea took place on 31 May 1916 when the cruiser and battleship fleets from both countries converged on the same area off the Jutland peninsula. Admiral Scheer, the overall commander of the German High Seas fleet, had devised a 'cunning plan'. In a desperate attempt to end British control of the sea and the blockade of Germany, Scheer planned to lure the British battle cruisers into a trap using his own cruiser fleet. However, Admiral Jellicoe, commander of the British Grand Fleet, had decoded the German message and come up with a plan of his own.

## The battle

Beatty arrived first off the coast of Jutland because his ships were faster and he had less distance to travel. His cruisers fought against the German cruisers led by Hipper. It soon became clear that the Germans could fire their guns more accurately and that there was something seriously wrong with the British ships. The armour plating on the gun turrets was too thin, which meant that they were easily destroyed by direct hits.

Two British cruisers blew up. Suddenly, the great battleships of Scheer's fleet arrived, and Beatty was in serious trouble. He turned north to lure Scheer towards Jellicoe's fleet. The Germans followed and fell into the trap as Jellicoe's fleet of dreadnoughts opened fire.

Admirals Scheer and Hipper, realising they had sailed into a trap, turned for home as night began to fall. German destroyers raced about making a smoke screen and threatening to mount a torpedo attack on Jellicoe's ships, so he did not chase them until it was too late. By the time morning came the Germans had escaped safely to port.

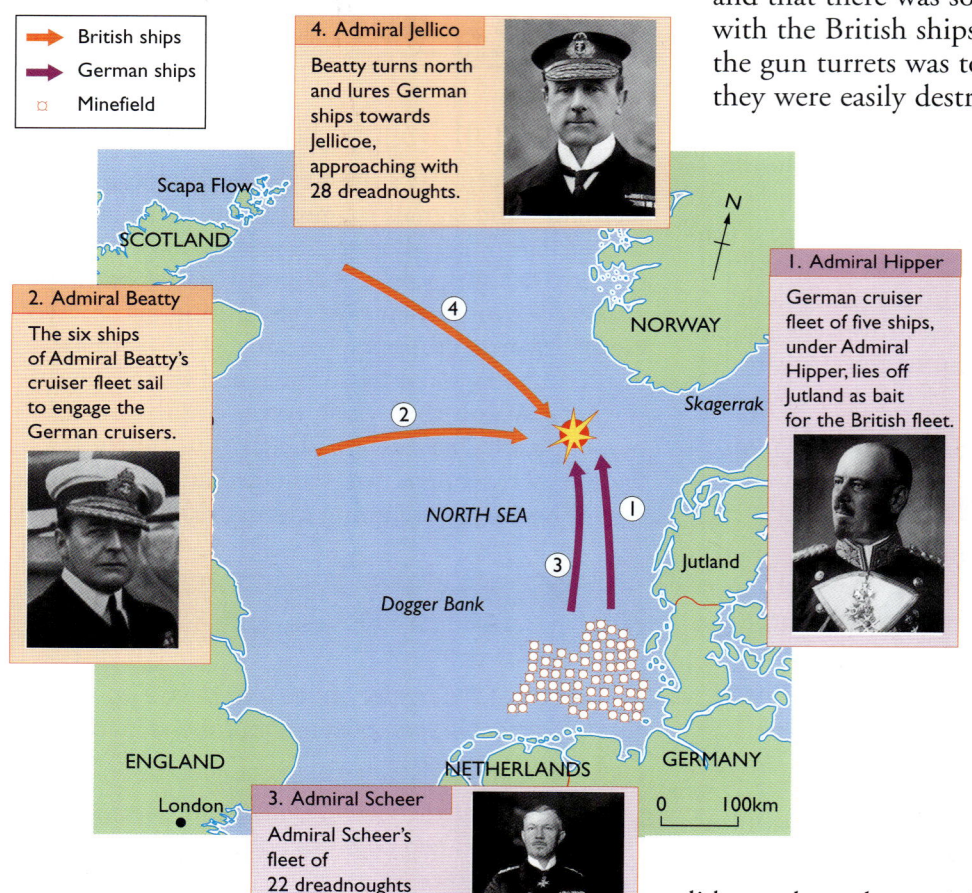

**Key:**
- British ships
- German ships
- Minefield

**1. Admiral Hipper**
German cruiser fleet of five ships, under Admiral Hipper, lies off Jutland as bait for the British fleet.

**2. Admiral Beatty**
The six ships of Admiral Beatty's cruiser fleet sail to engage the German cruisers.

**3. Admiral Scheer**
Admiral Scheer's fleet of 22 dreadnoughts join the battle.

**4. Admiral Jellico**
Beatty turns north and lures German ships towards Jellicoe, approaching with 28 dreadnoughts.

A map showing the Battle of Jutland

The War to End Wars 1914–1919

## Results of the battle
Both sides claimed victory, so who won the battle?

| The British war | The German war |
|---|---|
| • The Germans had fled the battle.<br><br>• The German fleet rarely went to sea again, leaving the Royal Navy in control of the North Sea.<br><br>• The British continued to blockade Germany. A US newspaper summarised the outcome of Jutland in this way: 'The German fleet has assaulted its jailor, but it is still in jail.'<br><br>• The Germans were forced to revert to unrestricted U-boat warfare (see page 53), which brought the USA into the war on the Allied side. | • The Germans had inflicted the greater losses, with fourteen British and only eleven German ships sunk.<br><br>• The British suffered far heavier casualties – 6000 British to 2500 German.<br><br>• German gunnery was far better – about half of all big shells scored hits compared with about a third of those fired by the British ships.<br><br>• The design of the German ships, especially the gun turrets, was shown to be superior. |

**Source A** A young lieutenant on Beatty's ship, HMS *Lion*, wrote about the problem of the gun turret

A bloodstained Sergeant of Marines appeared on the bridge. He was hatless, his clothes were burnt and he seemed to be somewhat dazed. I asked him what was the matter. He replied ' "Q" turret has gone, sir. All the crew are killed, and we have flooded the **magazine**.' I looked upon the bridge. The armoured roof of 'Q' turret had been folded back like a sardine tin.

**Source B** British newspaper headlines about Jutland, 1 June 1916, that exaggerated the German losses

> **ADMIRAL BEATTY FIGHTS THE WHOLE GERMAN FLEET**
> **COMPENSATION FOR OUR HEAVY LOSSES**
> Admiralty counts 18 German ships sunk against our 14

### The effects of the British blockade, 1917–18

The British blockade was far more effective during the final eighteen months of the war than it had been in the first two years. Denmark and Sweden agreed to limit their exports of dairy produce and iron ore to Germany. In addition the US entry into the war on the side of the Allies in April 1917 (see page 64) ended all trade with Germany. The blockade played an important role in Germany's eventual defeat.

- It left Germany seriously short of iron ore and chemicals, which it needed to manufacture weapons and poisonous gas.
- In the spring of 1918 Ludendorff gambled everything on outright victory before Germany was starved out of the war (see page 68).

Food shortages contributed greatly to the revolution that took place in Germany in October–November 1918 (see page 70).

## Tasks

1. What can you learn from Source A about the design of the British ships? (Remember how to answer this type of question? For further guidance, see page 18.)

2. How useful is Source B as evidence about the Battle of Jutland? (This is a utility question. For further guidance, see pages 42 and 50.)

3. With the aid of a sketch, describe the sequence of events before and during the battle. Use the map on page 36 to help with your sketch.

4. Where would you place the results of the battle on the following line? Explain your decision.

   British victory    Drawn battle    German victory

The war at sea and Gallipoli

# Why did the Allies launch the Gallipoli campaign?

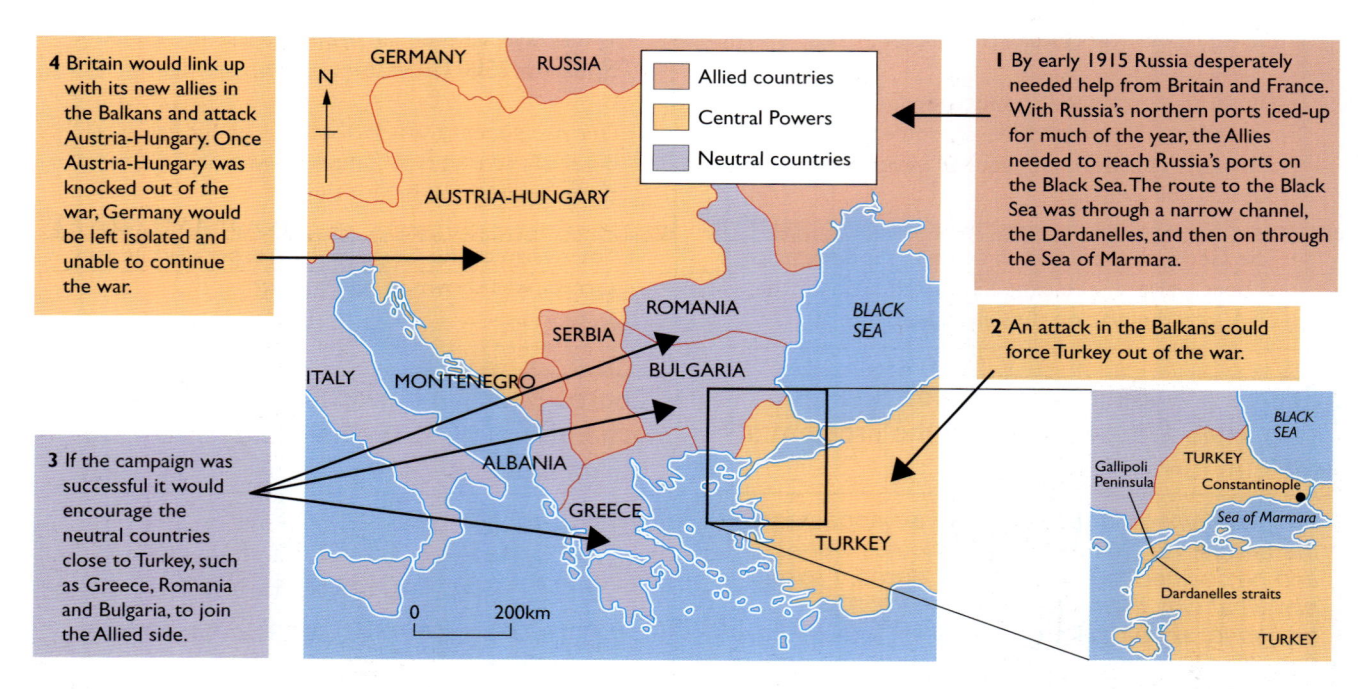

**4** Britain would link up with its new allies in the Balkans and attack Austria-Hungary. Once Austria-Hungary was knocked out of the war, Germany would be left isolated and unable to continue the war.

**1** By early 1915 Russia desperately needed help from Britain and France. With Russia's northern ports iced-up for much of the year, the Allies needed to reach Russia's ports on the Black Sea. The route to the Black Sea was through a narrow channel, the Dardanelles, and then on through the Sea of Marmara.

**2** An attack in the Balkans could force Turkey out of the war.

**3** If the campaign was successful it would encourage the neutral countries close to Turkey, such as Greece, Romania and Bulgaria, to join the Allied side.

Map showing the location and strategic importance of the Dardanelles and the aims of the Gallipoli campaign

In 1915 the Allies launched an offensive against Turkey, which had recently joined the Central Powers, on the Gallipoli peninsula. It was the idea of Winston Churchill, the **First Lord of the Admiralty**, who saw the attack at Gallipoli as a way of breaking the stalemate on the Western Front. He believed that if the Allies knocked the Turks out of the war they could open up an alternative front against Austria and Germany. The Germans would have to divert much-needed troops and resources from the Western Front.

At first the British and French could not spare troops from the Western Front. Churchill therefore proposed a naval campaign, with Allied ships sailing through the Dardanelles to the Turkish capital, Constantinople. The naval attack began on 18 March 1915. The Turks had put **mines** in the water, and three battleships were blown up, forcing the Allies to call off the campaign. It had failed because the Allies had not used proper minesweepers to clear the Dardanelles.

## The landings

The Allies now changed their plan to landings on the Gallipoli peninsula. Troops would be used to capture the Turkish forts that guarded the Dardanelles. They would attack the west coast of Gallipoli, cross overland and capture the forts from behind. It took several weeks to prepare the invasion as the Allies intended to use Australian and New Zealand Army Corps (ANZACs) who were diverted from Egypt. However, the Turks knew about the attack plan and had plenty of time to strengthen their position.

On 25 April 1915 British troops landed on five beaches at Cape Helles, while the Anzacs landed further north at a bay soon to be called Anzac Cove. However the Turks were ready on all beaches and mowed down thousands of advancing troops. With a great effort, the soldiers managed to secure a foothold on the beach and dig trenches to protect themselves.

The War to End Wars 1914–1919

In August the British tried further landings at Suvla Bay. These took the Turks unawares but the British commander delayed any advance, which gave the Turks the opportunity to send reinforcements and prevent any breakthrough.

### Source A A New Zealand soldier describes the landing at Anzac Cove

The whole beach went up in flames in front of us. Bullets hit us like a blizzard of lead. The boat next to us was torn apart – bodies, blood, splinters of wood. Bodies jammed so tight in other small boats they couldn't even fall.

### Source C John Masefield, who took part in the landings, describes the scene

From every rifle and machine gun began a murderous fire upon the ships and boats. There was no question of their missing. Many were killed in the water. Many who were wounded were swept away and drowned. Some reached the shore. These instantly doubled out to cut the wire entanglements and were killed. Only a handful reached cover.

### Source B A model showing the landing on Cape Helles beach, 25 April 1915

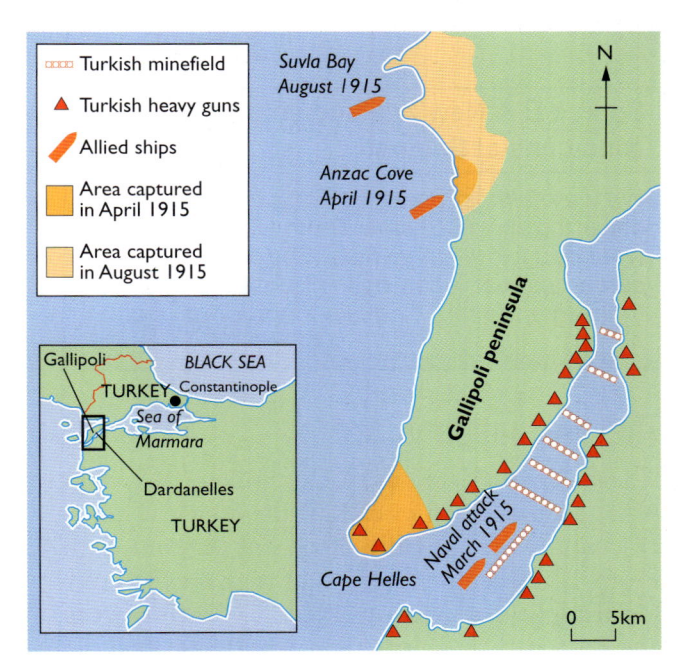

A map showing the Gallipoli landings

## Tasks

1. Look at the map on page 38. The Gallipoli campaign had several aims. Which do you think was the most important? Explain your choice.

2. What can you learn from Source A about the landings at Anzac Cove? (Remember how to answer this type of question? For further guidance, see page 18.)

3. Does Source C support the evidence of Sources A and B about the Gallipoli landings? (Remember how to answer this type of question? For further guidance see pages 30–31.)

4. If you were a military adviser, what advice would you give to the Allied commanders about:
a) the overall feasibility of the Gallipoli campaign
b) the Dardanelles campaign
c) the landings at Gallipoli?

The war at sea and Gallipoli

# Why did the Gallipoli campaign fail?

Once the troops had landed, they quickly dug trenches but were pinned down on the beaches by the Turkish defenders. A stalemate followed like the one on the Western Front.

## Conditions on the beaches

In summer the heat and dust were dreadful. Water was extremely scarce and had to be carried by mules in cans from ships. Flies were everywhere, smothering every scrap of food and causing widespread dysentery. Men soon grew weak and had to be sent to hospital ships offshore. Of seven Anzac battalions examined in September 1915, 78 per cent of the men had dysentery and 64 per cent had skin sores.

The area between the trenches was littered with dead bodies, rotting in the hot weather. When the stench became unbearable, the two sides agreed a **ceasefire** to bury the bodies.

However, conditions, if anything, got worse in the winter. The dust and heat turned to mud and snow. Water poured down the hills into Allied trenches. Blizzards swept over men without overcoats, huddled together for warmth and caking them with freezing mud and ice. The worst day was 28 November when the cold reached its worst and 15,000 died of exposure.

> **Source A** Memories from Second Lieutenant G. D. Horridge
>
> *After the battles of June 4 and 6, the land in between the trenches was covered with dead. Because of this and the hot sun, flies bred there until their number was horrendous. They attacked our food remorselessly. The contamination made everyone ill. Typhoid and dysentery were rife.*

Anzac Cove after the landings – the Anzacs dig in where they can

> **Source B** A New Zealand soldier describes conditions at Gallipoli
>
> *We were almost up to the firing line and I shall never forget what I saw. There were dead and wounded lying everywhere. The wounded were so numerous that it had been impossible to cope with them all and many had lain there for days.*

## The evacuation

The stalemate lasted until December 1915. The Allies then decided to call off the attack. The evacuation was the only success of the campaign. From 12 December, groups of men were secretly led at night from their trenches to waiting boats and ferried away. More than 83,000 escaped without a single death.

## Results of the campaign

Here are some of the results of the campaign.

- Turkey was not knocked out of the war.
- Bulgaria joined the war on the side of the Central Powers.
- Churchill resigned due to the campaign's failure.
- There were 213,000 Allied deaths.
- There were 300,000 Turkish deaths.

The campaign did have some minor achievements.

- The campaign diverted the Turks from their attack on Egypt and attempts to seize the Suez Canal.
- No troops died during the evacuation.
- A few British submarines sailed into the Black Sea and destroyed several Turkish warships.

## Reasons for failure

**Source C** Sir Maurice Hankey, a member of the British War Council, writing in late 1915

*No one had worked out how many soldiers and guns are needed to take Gallipoli from the Turks. We have just said that we can ship a certain number of soldiers there and that ought to be enough.*

**Source D** From the *Guinness Book of Military Blunders*, 1991

*Sir John French refused to allow his best commanders to be moved from France, where he felt the war would be decided. It is not surprising that in 'scraping the barrel' Lord Kitchener came up with the 'most abject collection of generals ever collected in one spot' to go with the out-of-date warships sent to the Dardanelles.*

**Source E** From a recent history of the Gallipoli campaign

*There was a lack of up-to-date knowledge about the Turkish positions. The instructions were vague and Lord Kitchener only had a hazy idea of what was needed. Hamilton's only intelligence consisted of a 1912 manual on the Turkish army, some old, inaccurate maps and a tourist guidebook.*

**Source F** A photograph of Turkish troops at Gallipoli

**Source G** Major H. Mynors Senior, writing about the Turks at Gallipoli

*The Turks had sited their trenches very cleverly. They dig like moles and prepare line after line for defence – seven or eight close behind the other. Johnny Turk was a formidable enemy who would die for his country.*

### Tasks

1. Examine the results of the campaign. Did the campaign achieve any of the aims (see page 38)?

2. Was the campaign a total failure? Give reasons for your answer.

3. a) Make a copy of the following table. Looking at Sources C–G, decide which interpretation of the failure of the Gallipoli campaign each source supports. Fill in the table giving reasons for your choices. An example has been done for you.

| The campaign failed due to the Turkish defenders | The campaign failed due to poor Allied leadership |
|---|---|
| Source G suggests that the Turks were a very strong enemy. | |

b) 'The main reason for the failure of the Gallipoli campaign was poor Allied leadership.' Use Sources C–G and your own knowledge to explain whether you agree with this view. Use your table from (a) to help you with your answer. (This is a synthesis question. For further guidance, see pages 74–76.)

The war at sea and Gallipoli

# Examination practice

The third question on Paper 2 is the utility question. It asks you to explain the utility of two sources – how useful they are in their contents and their Nature, Origin and Purpose (NOP). It is worth eight marks.

You will concentrate on the utility of contents in this section and look at the utility of the NOP in Chapter 4, page 50.

> **Source A** An Australian folk song
>
> *How well I remember that terrible day*
> *When the blood stained the sand and water*
> *And how in that hell called Suvla Bay*
> *We were butchered like lambs to the slaughter.*
> *Johnny Turk was ready*
> *He primed himself well*
> *He showered us with bullets and he rained us with shells*
> *And in five minutes flat he'd blown us to hell*
> *Nearly blew us right back to Australia.*

## Question 1 – Utility (content only)

How useful is Source A as evidence of the landings during the Gallipoli campaign? (8 marks)

## How to answer

The question is asking you what is useful about what the source is suggesting about the Gallipoli campaign.

- Decide, from your own knowledge of the topic, what is useful about what the source is suggesting.
- Always begin your answer with 'The source is useful because it suggests ...'

This shows the examiner that you are focusing on utility. One example has been done for you in the planning circle.

- What else is useful about what the source suggests?
- Make a copy of the planning circle and complete the 'have a go yourself' section.
- In what ways is the content or what the source suggests limited? For example, it could be:
  – giving a very one-sided view – what is it?
  – a view that is inaccurate or untypical
  – a view that omits important factors.

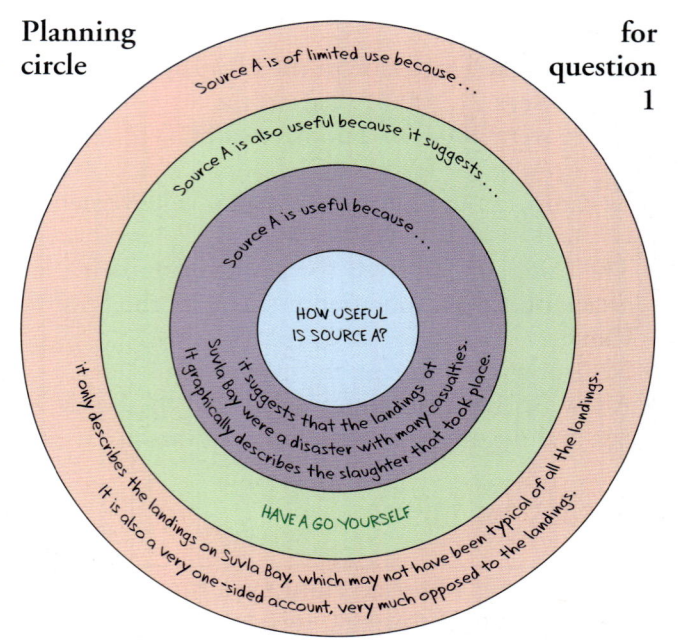

**Planning circle for question 1**

*Source A is of limited use because...*
*Source A is also useful because it suggests...*
*Source A is useful because...*

**HOW USEFUL IS SOURCE A?**

*it suggests that the landings at Suvla Bay were a disaster with many casualties.*
*It graphically describes the slaughter that took place.*

**HAVE A GO YOURSELF**

*It is also a very one-sided account, very much opposed to the landings.*
*it only describes the landings on Suvla Bay, which may not have been typical of all the landings.*

- Again, begin your answer with 'The source is of limited use because ...'. Look at the example done for you in the outer circle.

> **Source B** A British soldier who took part in the landings at Suvla Bay
>
> *We were loaded into small boats and rowed towards the shores of Suvla Bay where we had to wade ashore for about 50 metres as the boats couldn't get in any nearer owing to the shallow water. The Turks had spotted the landing and opened up fire. We were scared out of our wits. Then we began to look around for our officers for further orders, but there were no officers near us. It appeared that they had been landed on another beach. We waited round all day for orders.*

## Question 2 – Utility (content only)

How useful is Source B as evidence of the landings at Suvla Bay? (8 marks)

## Now have a go yourself

- Use a planning circle to plan your answer.
- Write up your answer. Try to write 2 paragraphs:
  – one on the utility of the contents
  – one on the limitations of the contents.

# 4 The impact of technology on the war

**Source A** An aerial photograph of a French gas attack on German lines in Belgium, 1916

### Task

*What can you learn about a gas attack from Source A? (Remember how to answer this type of question? For further guidance, see page 18.)*

After the failure of the Schlieffen Plan in 1914, the Great War on the Western Front became a defensive conflict, which turned into a **war of attrition**. However, during the war, there were several attempts to break the stalemate with the introduction of new weapons such as gas, tanks and aeroplanes. Though each of these weapons scored some successes, none was able to give one side a clear advantage and permit a breakthrough. The stalemate continued until 1918.

This chapter answers the following questions:

- How was gas used on the Western Front?
- How were tanks used on the Western Front?
- How did U-boats threaten Britain?
- How was Britain able to overcome the threat of the U-boats?
- What changes took place in the war in the air?

## Source skills

This chapter gives you guidance on the third source question on Paper 2. This is the utility question, which asks you to decide the usefulness of two sources. It is worth eight marks. In Chapter 3 you looked at the utility of the contents of a source (see page 42). In this chapter you will concentrate on the Nature, Origin and Purpose (NOP) of a source.

# How was gas used on the Western Front?

**Source A** French cavalry and horse wearing gas masks

**Source B** From the memoirs of a soldier in the British army, here writing about a gas attack in 1916

*I was sitting on the fire step, cleaning my rifle, when one of the new lot called out to me: 'There's a sort of greenish, yellow cloud rolling along the ground out in front, it's coming...'*

*But I didn't wait for him to finish. I grabbed my bayonet, which was detached from the rifle and I gave the alarm by banging a nearby empty shell case. At the same instant, gongs started ringing down the trench, the signal for all the soldiers to put on their respirators, or smoke helmets, as we call them. For a minute, there was chaos in our trench – soldiers adjusting their helmets, some running here and there, and others turning out of the dugouts with fixed bayonets, to man the fire step.*

### Task

1. What can you learn from Source A about the use of gas in the First World War? (Remember how to answer this type of question? For further guidance, see page 18.)

## Early use of gas

Gas was used as early as August 1914, when the French decided to deploy **tear gas** against the Germans as they advanced through Belgium. The gas was meant to slow the German soldiers but it failed to be an active deterrent because it did not kill, nor did it cause panic. The German retaliation came in October when they shelled French positions with a gas that caused violent sneezing attacks. The intention was not to kill the enemy, but to permit a breakthrough by making the enemy unable to defend a position. The gas simply failed to harm the enemy.

## Types of gas

The first time that a poisonous gas was used in the war was at the Second Battle of Ypres in April 1915, where the Germans deployed chlorine against the French. The French thought that the Germans were advancing behind a smokescreen and therefore stood ready to repel the attackers. When the gas reached them there was instant terror and they ran away. However, the Germans did not anticipate such a rapid retreat and were unable to capitalise on their initial success.

After this development, each side introduced more devastating chemicals and by 1918 more than 63 different types of poisonous gas had been used. By 1918 the use of poison gases had become widespread, particularly on the Western Front. The German army ended the war as the heaviest user of gas. It has been estimated that the Germans used 68,000 tons of gas and the French and British 36,000 and 25,000 tons respectively. After about May 1915 deaths from gas were relatively rare but each side continued to use it because it injured soldiers and also created great disruption.

The War to End Wars 1914–1919

| Gas | Effects | Advantages | Disadvantages |
|---|---|---|---|
| Chlorine (first used April 1915) | Choking, damaged the lungs, victims' lungs filled and they died of drowning. | • When first used it caused tremendous panic.<br>• Killed the enemy. | • Visible and soldiers were able to prepare for its arrival.<br>• Did not kill in huge numbers.<br>• Wind could disperse it or blow it back towards the side that had released it. |
| Phosgene (first used December 1915) | • Soldiers inhaled large amounts and lungs were damaged as a result.<br>• Killed the enemy. | Did not have a strong smell as chlorine did, therefore soldiers inhaled large amounts before realising it was there. | • Did not kill in huge numbers.<br>• Often carried in chlorine gas and could be dispersed or returned by the wind. |
| Mustard gas (often called Yperite, first used against the Russians in September 1917) | • Blistering of skin, flesh eaten away, vomiting, sore eyes, internal and external bleeding, blindness.<br>• Death could result up to five weeks after exposure to the gas. | Almost odourless, colourless. It was more difficult to protect soldiers against this gas than against other types. | • It remained active in the soil for weeks after release, which made the capture of infected trenches a dangerous task.<br>• Did not kill in huge numbers.<br>• Took twelve hours to take effect. |

Table of main gases used during the war

### Source C From the poem 'Dulce et decorum est' by Wilfred Owen, a British soldier and poet who was killed on 4 November 1918

*Gas! Gas! Quick, boys!*
*An ecstasy of fumbling,*
*Fitting the clumsy helmets just in time;*
*But someone still was yelling out and stumbling,*
*And flound'ring like a man in fire or lime . . .*
*Dim, through the misty panes and thick green light,*
*As under a green sea, I saw him drowning.*
*In all my dreams, before my helpless sight,*
*He plunges at me, guttering, choking, drowning.*

### Tasks

2. Does Source C support the evidence of Source B about a gas attack? (Remember how to answer this type of question? For further guidance, see pages 30–31.)

3. Source C is a poem. How useful is this source in helping you to understand a gas attack? (This is a utility question. For further guidance, see pages 42 and 50.)

4. Work in pairs. Make a list of suggestions to explain why deaths from gas after 1915 'were relatively rare'.

5. What can you learn from the table of casualties about the effects of gas in the First World War? (Remember how to answer this type of question? For further guidance, see page 18.)

| Country | Total casualties | Deaths |
|---|---|---|
| Austria-Hungary | 100,000 | 3,000 |
| British empire | 188,706 | 8,109 |
| France | 190,000 | 8,000 |
| Germany | 200,000 | 9,000 |
| Italy | 60,000 | 4,627 |
| Russia | 419,340 | 56,000 |
| USA | 72,807 | 1,462 |

Table showing the casualties caused by gas in the First World War

The impact of technology on the war

## Protection against gases

Gradually, each army developed means of combating the use of gas. Initially, simple methods were used, and soldiers were even advised that holding a urine-drenched cloth over their face would serve in an emergency to protect against the effects of chlorine. In 1915, British soldiers were given efficient gas masks, but these were not really effective when the Germans began using mustard gas, because this gas attacked the skin. By 1918 soldiers on both sides were far better prepared to meet the ever-present threat of a gas attack. **Filter respirators** were standard and proved highly effective.

### Tasks

*6. Why did gas fail to bring about the breakthrough that the army leaders had hoped for?*

*7. You are a doctor/nurse on the Western Front. Write a letter home describing your experiences of being involved in helping soldiers after a gas attack.*

*8. How useful is Source D as evidence of the use of gas in the First World War? (This is a utility question. For further guidance, see pages 42 and 50.)*

**Source D** An official photograph of British gas casualties, taken in 1918

The War to End Wars 1914–1919

# How were tanks used on the Western Front?

Source A Official photograph of a British tank going into action at Flers during the Battle of the Somme, September 1916

### Tasks

1. What can you learn about the tanks in the First World War from Source A? (Remember how to answer this type of question? For further guidance, see page 18.)

2. How useful is Source A as evidence of a tank attack in the First World War? (This is a utility question. For further guidance, see pages 42 and 50.)

## The first use of tanks

Tanks were first used by British forces in September 1916 at the Battle of the Somme but had only limited success. During the next two years they continued to experience mixed fortunes but in the summer of 1918, they did play an important role in the Allied breakthrough of the German lines.

The British wanted a machine that could cross a trench and break through barbed wire. It was specified that any armour plating would have to protect the tank from small arms fire. The first tank was ready for action in early 1916 but it was only by September that there were enough to use in an attack. However, their initial use created tension in the army. The British commander-in-chief, Haig, decided to use them against the wishes of the commander of the tank corps, who wanted to use tanks only when the army had huge numbers of the new machines. Haig wanted to use the first fifty immediately because he wanted to be able to boast some success in the Battle of the Somme. As commander-in-chief, his decision was final.

The impact of technology on the war

## The Battle of Flers

On 15 September 1916, 49 tanks began the attack at Flers. Seventeen tanks broke down on the way to the British lines; another nine failed to work when the attack began and five others became stuck in ditches. Eighteen tanks moved slowly into no man's land and were able to capture their objectives. Many Germans ran away, terrified of the new weapon. Over the next three days, gains of over four miles were made on a narrow front. However, bad weather, shortage of tanks and increased German reinforcements meant that the initial successes could not be built on.

**Source B** A comment made after the action at Flers by Winston Churchill, who had played an important role in encouraging the development of tanks

*My poor land battleships have been used prematurely on a petty scale.*

**Source C** From an article in the *Manchester Guardian*, 18 September 1916, describing the tank attack at Flers

*You must imagine this huge engine stalking majestically amid the ruins, followed by the infantry, drawing the disarmed Germans from their holes in the ground like a magnet ... our chaps laughed instead of killing them. Before turning back, the tank silenced a battery of artillery, captured its gunners, and handed them over to the infantry. Finally, the tank retraced its steps to the old British line at the close of a profitable day. The German officers captured in Flers have not yet taken in the scene – the 'High Street' and the cheering bomb-throwers marching behind the travelling fort, which displayed on one armoured side the startling placard, 'Great Hun Defeat. Extra Special!'*

## Problems faced by tanks

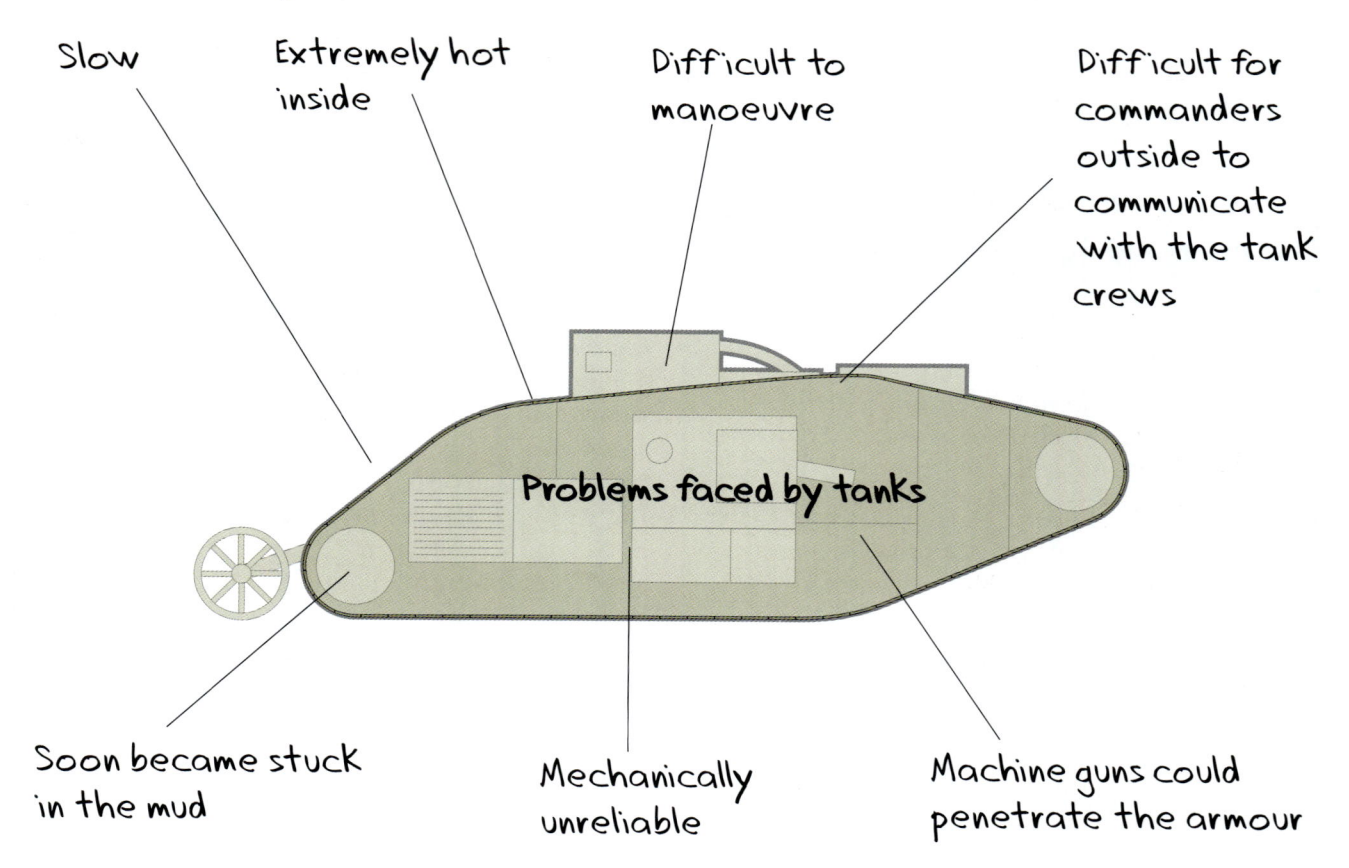

- Slow
- Extremely hot inside
- Difficult to manoeuvre
- Difficult for commanders outside to communicate with the tank crews
- Soon became stuck in the mud
- Mechanically unreliable
- Machine guns could penetrate the armour

The War to End Wars 1914–1919

## Tanks in the later stages of the war

The first major success for the tank came at the Battle of Cambrai in November 1917, when the entire British Tank Corps of 474 tanks was involved in action against the Germans. The tanks broke through the German lines, and the supporting infantry was able to capture 10,000 German prisoners, 123 guns and 281 machine guns. The success of the tanks was not sustained because there were insufficient infantry reserves to follow up the breakthrough that had been achieved.

In the **August 1918 offensive**, 604 tanks assisted an Allied advance of 32 kilometres on the Western Front. Yet even here the tanks' problems had not been overcome, as Source D indicates.

**Source D** A graph showing the number of tanks in working order at the Battle of Amiens, 8–12 August 1918

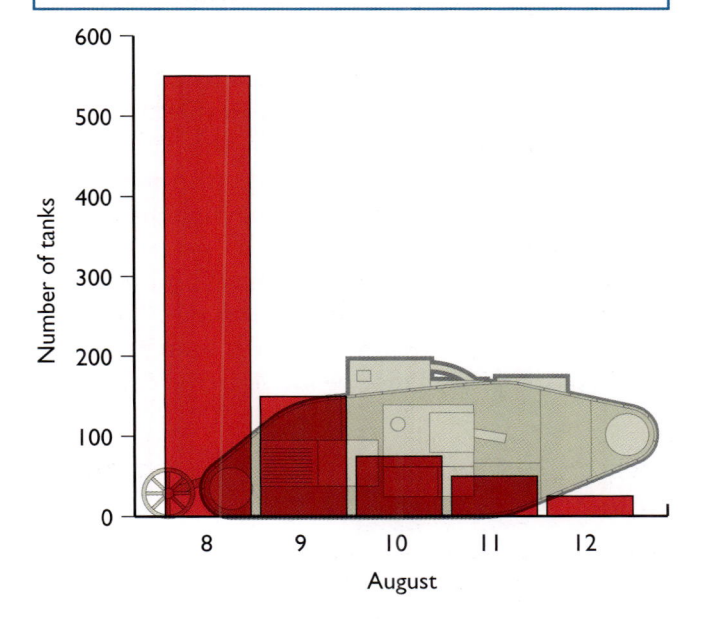

| Year | UK | France | Germany | Italy | USA |
|---|---|---|---|---|---|
| 1916 | 150 | – | – | – | – |
| 1917 | 1,277 | 800 | – | – | – |
| 1918 | 1,391 | 4,000 | 20 | 6 | 84 |

A table showing tank production, 1916–18

## Tasks

3. Work in groups to produce a case for or against the use of tanks in the First World War.

4. Study Sources A (page 47) and C (page 48). Does Source A support Source C about tank attacks in the First World War? (Remember how to answer this type of question? For further guidance, see pages 30–31.)

5. Look at Source B. What point was Churchill making?

6. What can you learn from Source D about tanks in the First World War? (Remember how to answer this type of question? For further guidance, see page 18.)

7. Study the table of tank production. What does this table show about the use of tanks in the First World War?

The impact of technology on the war

# Examination practice

Chapter 3 (page 42) explained how to evaluate the utility of the *contents* of a source. In this chapter we will concentrate on the NOP – the Nature, Origin and Purpose of each source. You must analyse these aspects to achieve the highest marks (7/8 marks).

In order to reach higher-level marks for this question you have to explain the value (usefulness) and limitations of the NOP of each source. This is found in the **provenance** of the source – the information given above or below it. A good tip is to highlight or underline keywords in the provenance that show either the utility or the limitations of the source. An example of how you could approach this is given for Source A below.

## Question 1 – utility

How useful is Source A as evidence of the problems facing tanks in the First World War?

### Utility

**Nature** – This is a report, which suggests it is useful because it would have been sent to the officer's superiors and he would be under orders to give an accurate account.

**Origin** – The date and the writer suggest the source is useful because it was written by someone who actually experienced early tank warfare. It is an eyewitness account.

**Purpose** – This is useful because it is quite a critical account of the tank, made at a time when solutions were being sought to the war of attrition.

### Limitations

**Nature** – There is nothing to indicate to whom the report was sent, or if it was sent at all, which limits its usefulness.

**Origin** – The source only gives the view of one officer, which may not be typical. It was written early in the development of tanks and improvements were made by 1918.

**Purpose** – This also has limitations. The writer may have exaggerated the effects in order to convince potential readers that tanks were not the key to the future.

> **Source A** An officer's report of 1916, describing the effects on the tank crews of being inside tanks during a battle
>
> *The pulses of one crew were taken immediately they got out of their tank. The heart rate averaged 130 to the minute or just twice as fast as it should have been. Two men of one crew lost their reason and had to be restrained by force, and one tank commander became delirious. In some cases where infantry were carried in the tank, they fainted within three-quarters of an hour of the start of the approach to the lines.*

NOP means:

**N** Nature of the source
What type of source is it? A speech, a photograph, a cartoon, a letter, an extract from a diary? How will the nature of the source affect its utility? For example, a private letter is often very useful because the person who wrote it generally gives their honest views.

**O** Origin of the source
Who wrote or produced the source? Are their views worth knowing? Are they giving a one-sided view? When was it produced? It could be an eyewitness account. What are the advantages and disadvantages of eyewitness accounts?

**P** Purpose of the source
For what reason was the source produced? For example, the purpose of an advert is to make you buy a product. People usually make speeches to win your support. How does the purpose of the source affect its utility?

## Question 2 – utility
How useful is Source B as evidence of the role of tanks in the First World War?

Source B An official photograph taken in 1916 of a British tank crossing a shell crater (the wheels at the rear of the tank are the steering gear)

## Now have a go yourself
Include the utility and limitations of both the contents and the NOP of the source. If you need further guidance on this, look back to page 42 (Chapter 3).

Make a copy of the table opposite and use it to plan your answer.

|  | Value | Limitations |
|---|---|---|
| Contents |  |  |
| Nature |  |  |
| Origin |  |  |
| Purpose |  |  |

## The utility of two sources

In the examination you will be asked to explain the utility of two sources.

## Question 3 – utility

How useful are Sources C and D as evidence of new weapons in the First World War?

(8 marks)

**Source C** Photograph of a Canadian soldier with mustard gas burns, 1917

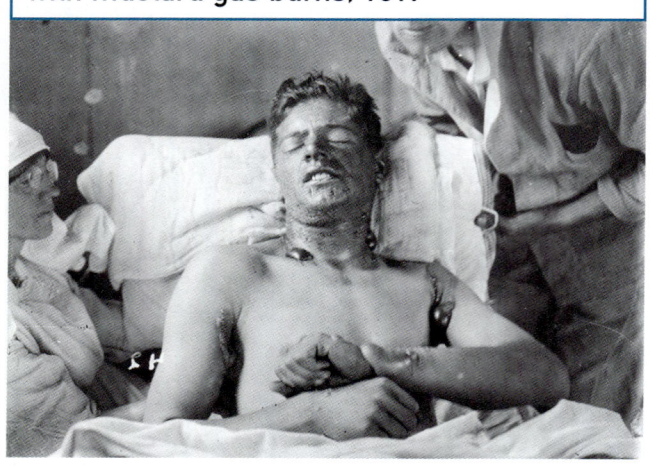

**Source D** From *Military Operations: France and Belgium, 1918* by Brigadier-General Sir James E. Edmonds, 1947

*The effect of tanks was really only on the morale of the soldiers. Tanks did a good service in crushing machine gun posts and in village fighting. They were less effective in moving across muddy territory where there were huge craters and damaged trenches. From what I saw, it was clear that the infantry liked to see them. Moreover, the enemy constantly exaggerated the numbers that were employed and often reported their presence when there was none. It is evident that the Germans stood in fear of tanks.*

## How to answer

- Explain the utility (value) and limitations of the contents of each source.
- Explain the utility and limitations of the NOP of each source.
- In your conclusion give a final judgement on the relative value of each source. For example, one source might provide one view of an event and the other a different view.

Make a copy of the following grid and use it to plan your answer.

| Source C | Utility | Limitations |
|---|---|---|
| Contents | | |
| Nature | | |
| Origin | | |
| Purpose | | |
| **Source D** | | |
| Contents | | |
| Nature | | |
| Origin | | |
| Purpose | | |

Here is a writing frame to help you:

Source C is useful because (contents) … etc.
.............................................................
Moreover, Source C is also useful because of (NOP)..................................................
Source C has limitations including (contents)..
.............................................................
Source C is also of limited use because (NOP)..
.............................................................
Source D is useful because (contents) … etc.
.............................................................
Moreover, Source D is also useful because of (NOP).................................................
Source D has limitations including (contents)..
.............................................................
Source D is also of limited use because (NOP).
.............................................................
In conclusion, Sources C and D are useful because they......................................

# How did U-boats threaten Britain?

**Source A** Cartoon published in the *Daily Mirror* on 10 May 1915, after the sinking of the *Lusitania*. The cartoon shows Germany above a gang of cut-throats including the Roman emperor Nero and King Herod. '*Deutschland über alles*' means 'Germany above all others'

## Task

*What message is the cartoonist putting across about Germany after the sinking of the* Lusitania?

The Germans were quick to use new technology in the war at sea. They used the submarine, or *Unterseeboot* (in English shortened to U-boat), to great effect for the first three years of the war. U-boats sank four British naval vessels in September 1914, three of those in one day, and these losses sent shock waves through Britain's naval command. By the end of 1914, eight warships and ten **merchant ships** had been sunk for the loss of five U-boats. It was the sinking of merchant ships that especially concerned the British government because vital food supplies were lost.

In February 1915 the German government decided to broaden its attacks on merchant ships. There were about 15,000 sailings each week to and from British ports, and the Germans felt they had to try to cripple the British war effort. They indicated that U-boats would attack any ship, regardless of which country it came from, in British waters. This was known as unrestricted submarine warfare. The threat to British food and other supplies from the USA was evident, and Britain could only continue the war if it received sufficient supplies from overseas.

The passenger ship *Lusitania* was sunk in May 1915 with the loss of 1198 lives, some of whom were US citizens. There was an outcry against the barbaric action towards civilians; the Germans scaled back their action. The *Lusitania* was in fact a valid target because it had been carrying ammunition but this was not disclosed at the time.

The U-boats continued to have great success in 1915, and in August that year they sank 185,000 tons of shipping. The tonnage of British shipping lost now exceeded the tonnage produced by the shipyards. In February 1917 Germany decided to begin unrestricted submarine warfare again in the hope of bringing Britain to its knees. It was a gamble because there was always the chance that the USA might enter the war if US vessels were attacked on a regular basis. If that were to happen, Germany gambled that it would be able to strangle the Allied supply line before the Americans could train and transport a large army.

The Germans had great successes in 1917, and by April Britain had only six weeks' food supply left. However, despite huge losses, the food shortages were eventually overcome, mainly as a result of the **convoy system**.

The impact of technology on the war

# How was Britain able to overcome the threat of the U-boats?

## The introduction of Q ships

By November 1914 British naval chiefs were concerned at the rate of losses from U-boat attacks. The idea of Q ships was put forward. These were old British steamers armed with hidden guns and torpedoes and, because they were loaded with wooden caskets, wood or cork, they were almost unsinkable. The idea was to attract the U-boat close to the ship and then remove the gun coverings and shell the U-boat as quickly as possible. By the end of the war there were about two hundred Q ships; they had sunk fourteen U-boats at a cost of 27 of the Q ships.

## Convoys

The U-boat threat was overcome in 1917 by the introduction of convoys. Merchant ships would travel in large numbers under the protection of naval destroyers. Destroyers used **depth charges** to attack U-boats and this new weapon did fend off the attackers. Although U-boats continued to sink ships, the losses were gradually reduced, and the threat of starvation that Britain faced in mid-1917 receded.

**Source A** Charles Pears' painting of Q ship *Schooner* attacking U-boat 93. Pears was the official artist for the navy. This picture was published in the *Illustrated London News* in December 1918

The War to End Wars 1914–1919

**Source B** A graph showing losses of Allied merchant ships in 1917, to nearest 1000 tons

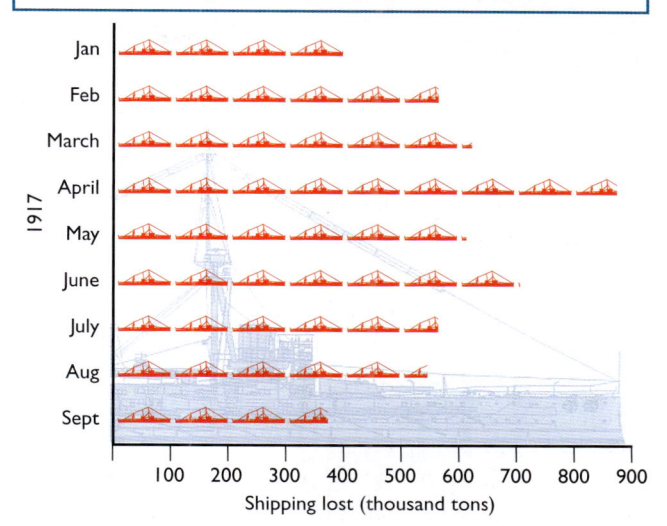

A German newspaper article from 22 September 1914, announcing the sinking of three Allied ships by U-boats in the North Sea (*an einem Tag* means 'in one day')

**Source C** A painting of a British convoy by Charles Pears, completed in 1918

## Tasks

1. How useful is Source A as evidence of Q ships in the First World War? (Remember how to answer this type of question? For further guidance, see pages 42 and 50.)

2. What can you learn from Source B about losses of Allied ships in 1917? (Remember how to answer this type of question? For further guidance, see page 18.)

3. Study Source C. What message is Source C trying to put across about convoys?

The impact of technology on the war

55

# What changes took place in the war in the air?

**Source A** Graph showing aircraft production during the First World War

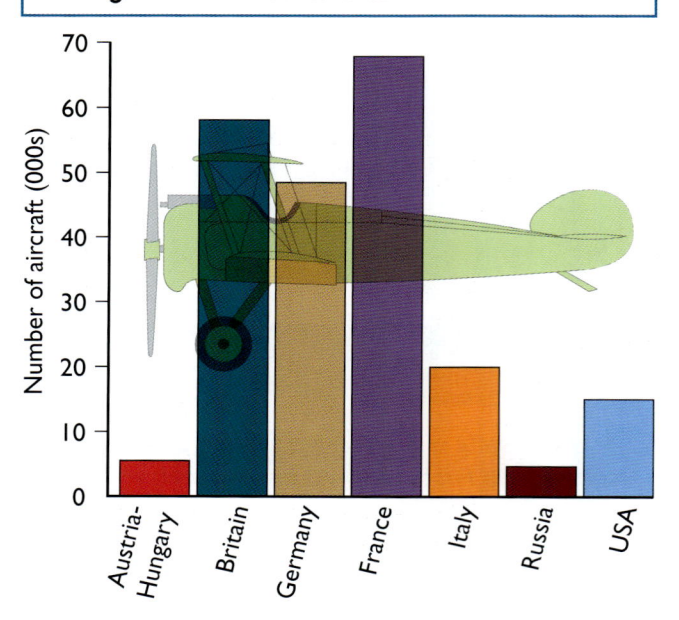

also used them as bombers, bringing terror to parts of south-east England.

## The work of aircraft on the Western Front

Aircraft could perform a range of tasks, as the diagram below shows. However, they were slow and could not carry large numbers of bombs. At first, pilots had to use pistols or revolvers to defend themselves, but eventually machine guns that could fire between the propeller blades were developed. Aircraft were often unreliable and could easily be shot down – Britain lost 1,270, for example, in the period March–May 1917. Aircraft were used against soldiers in the trenches but the aeroplane was not the weapon that brought an end to the stalemate.

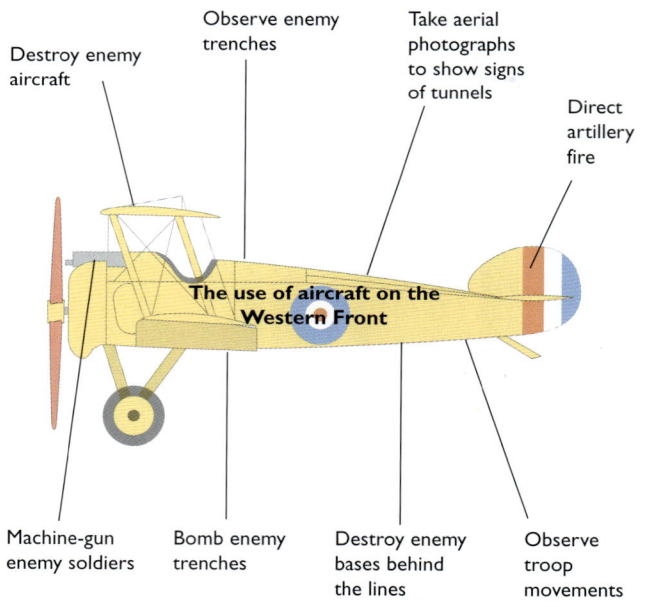

The use of aircraft on the Western Front:
- Destroy enemy aircraft
- Observe enemy trenches
- Take aerial photographs to show signs of tunnels
- Direct artillery fire
- Machine-gun enemy soldiers
- Bomb enemy trenches
- Destroy enemy bases behind the lines
- Observe troop movements

### Task

1. What can you learn from Source A about the use of aircraft in the First World War? (Remember how to answer this type of question? For further guidance, see page 18.)

When war broke out in 1914, aeroplanes were still in their infancy. The first flight had only been made in 1903, and military aircraft development was slow because civilian and military leaders did not think of aeroplanes as war machines. Source A shows that huge numbers of aircraft were built during the war; however, they did not become a really effective weapon. There were hints at the potential of air warfare towards the end of the war, when aeroplanes were used to support tank attacks at the Battle of Cambrai (see map on page 68) and also in the 1918 summer offensive. The Germans

## Pilots

Almost all the pilots involved in flying aircraft in the First World War were under the age of twenty-five. Many were under twenty-one, and most were sent into combat after about thirty hours of training. The life expectancy of a pilot at the front was quite short.

The War to End Wars 1914–1919

**Source B** A crashed British First World War plane

**Source C** A graph showing aircraft lost in combat during the First World War

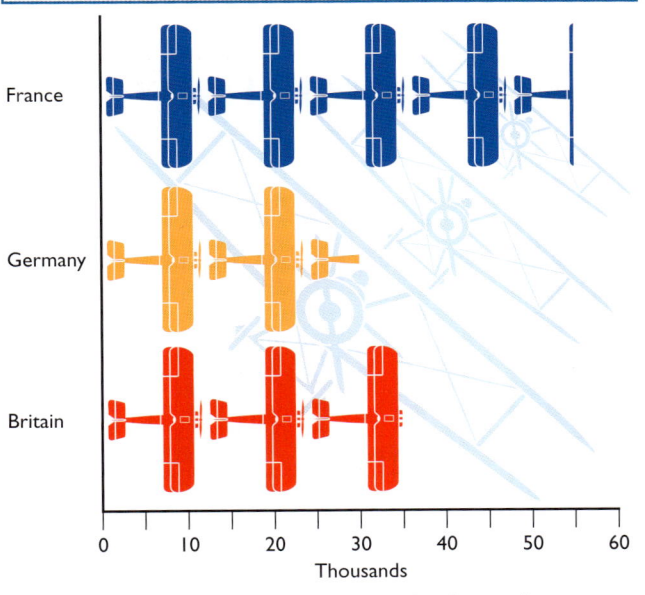

France
Germany
Britain

0   10   20   30   40   50   60
         Thousands
Aircraft lost (to nearest five thousand)

## Tasks

**2.** Look at the diagram that shows the uses of aircraft on page 56. Place the uses in order of importance and explain why you rank them so.

**3.** What can you learn about aeroplanes in the First World War from Source B? (Remember how to answer this type of question? For further guidance, see page 18.)

## Tasks

**4.** How useful is Source C as evidence about the use of aeroplanes in the First World War? (Remember how to answer this type of question? For further guidance, see pages 42 and 50.)

**5.** Re-read this chapter. Copy out the table below. For each of the weapons, give a mark out of ten based on its overall effectiveness and usefulness in the war. Then explain in what ways each was useful/effective.

|  | Mark out of 10 | Effective |
|---|---|---|
| **Gas** | | |
| **Tanks** | | |
| **U-boats** | | |
| **Aeroplanes** | | |

**6.** 'New weapons were of little use in the First World War.' Use Sources B (page 44), D (page 49), B (page 55) and C (page 57) and your own knowledge to explain whether you agree with this view. (This is a synthesis question. For further guidance, see pages 74–76.)

The impact of technology on the war

57

# Examination practice

**Source A** An artist's impression of British planes attacking German trenches, published in the *Sphere*, a British newspaper, 5 October 1918. The caption in the newspaper read: 'The machines dive on their target pouring out a storm of machine gun bullets, and at intervals release a bomb which falls with tremendous effect on the men below. The work is dangerous and our machines frequently return with their frames and fabrics riddled with bullets.'

**Source B** An official photograph of a British tank at the Battle of Passchendaele, 1917

## Question 1 – utility

How useful are Sources A and B as evidence of the effectiveness of new weapons in the First World War?

(8 marks)

Make a copy of the table below and use it to plan your answer.

| Source A | Value | Limitations |
|---|---|---|
| Contents | | |
| Nature | | |
| Origin | | |
| Purpose | | |
| **Source B** | | |
| Contents | | |
| Nature | | |
| Origin | | |
| Purpose | | |

# 5 The defeat of Germany, 1917–18

> **Source A** From *War in the Trenches* by M. Holden, written in 1973
>
> Once the Americans were in the war, the result was almost certain to be German defeat. The United States had vast supplies of manpower and materials, far greater than Germany had. Germany became exhausted; so too did France and Britain – but they could be boosted by the USA. And yet the Germans continued to attack. This weakened them. The Allies struck back, greatly aided by the newly arrived American support.

> **Task**
>
> What can you learn from Source A about the entry of the USA into the First World War? (Remember how to answer this type of question? For further guidance, see page 18.)

Events in 1917 changed the complexion of the First World War. In April the USA entered the war on Britain's side, following Germany's decision to resume unrestricted submarine warfare. Germany thought that the U-boats would be able to starve Britain to the point of surrender before the USA was able to have influence on the war. The **Bolshevik** Revolution in Russia in October resulted in the withdrawal of that country from the war. The loss of Russia was crucial because it meant that Germany was able to transfer men from the Eastern to the Western Front. Nevertheless, an end to the fighting was not anticipated. The German **Spring Offensive** of 1918 failed, and the Allies pushed back German forces during the summer, but the German collapse in October and early November was completely unexpected.

This chapter answers the following questions:

- Why did Russia withdraw from the war in 1917?
- Why and with what effect did the USA enter the war in 1917?
- What was the Spring Offensive and why did it fail?
- How and why did Germany collapse in 1918?

## Source skills

This chapter gives you guidance on the fourth source question on Paper 2 – the synthesis question. This question asks you to use the sources and your own knowledge to discuss an interpretation. The question is worth twelve marks.

# Why did Russia withdraw from the war in 1917?

## Why did Russia join the war?

When the heir to the Austrian throne, the Archduke Franz Ferdinand, was assassinated on 28 June 1914, Austria, supported by Germany, declared war on the Serbs. Serbia was allied to Russia, so the first reason why Russia joined the war in August 1914 was to help Serbia. Secondly, Russia also went to war to support France and Britain. All three countries were members of the Triple Entente.

Within Russia, there was tremendous enthusiasm for the war. Russia mobilised its troops more quickly than Germany had anticipated, which meant that Germany then had to fight on two fronts – Western and Eastern (see the Schlieffen Plan on pages 10–11). The main events of the war on the Eastern Front are shown on the map below.

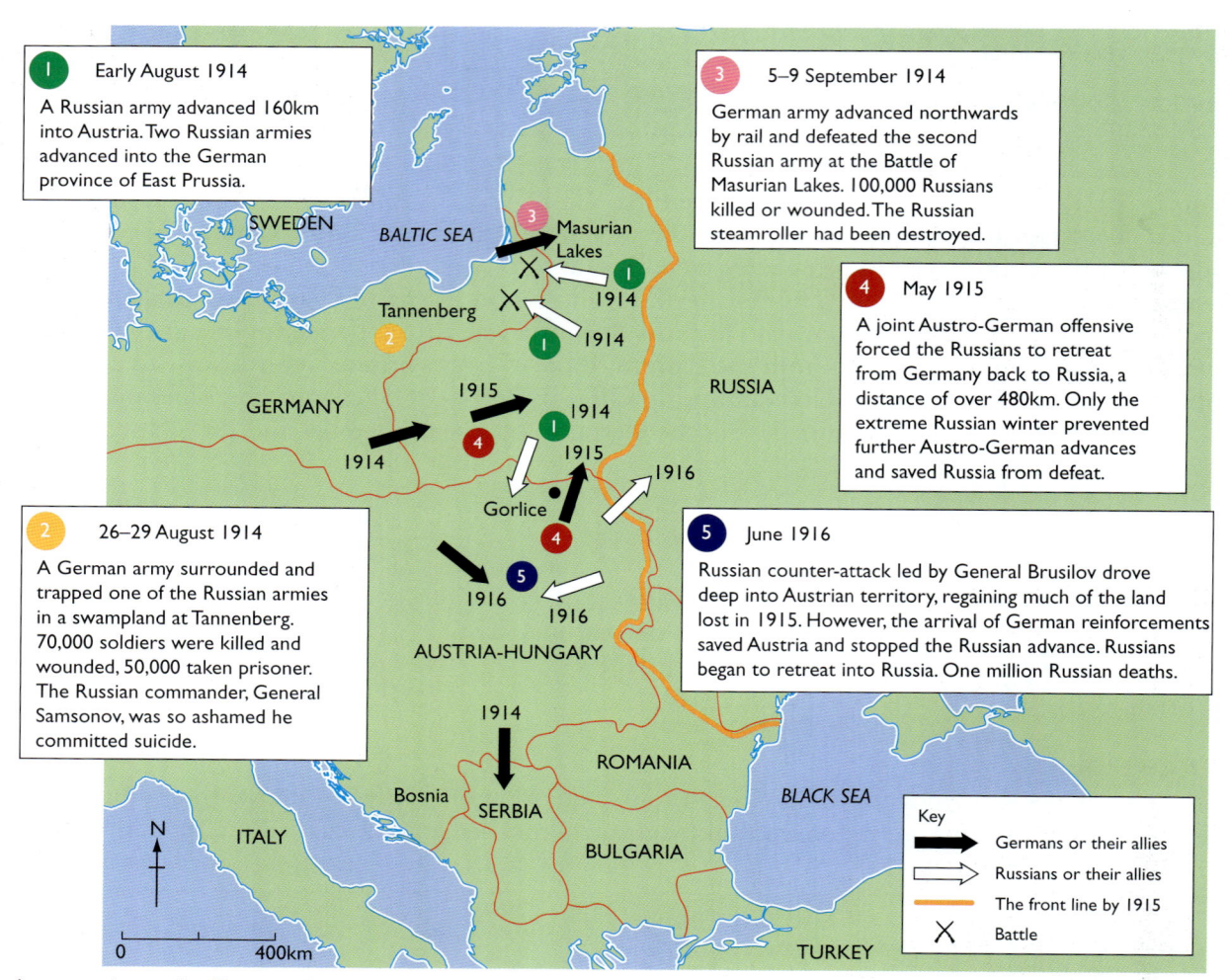

**1 Early August 1914**
A Russian army advanced 160km into Austria. Two Russian armies advanced into the German province of East Prussia.

**3 5–9 September 1914**
German army advanced northwards by rail and defeated the second Russian army at the Battle of Masurian Lakes. 100,000 Russians killed or wounded. The Russian steamroller had been destroyed.

**4 May 1915**
A joint Austro-German offensive forced the Russians to retreat from Germany back to Russia, a distance of over 480km. Only the extreme Russian winter prevented further Austro-German advances and saved Russia from defeat.

**2 26–29 August 1914**
A German army surrounded and trapped one of the Russian armies in a swampland at Tannenberg. 70,000 soldiers were killed and wounded, 50,000 taken prisoner. The Russian commander, General Samsonov, was so ashamed he committed suicide.

**5 June 1916**
Russian counter-attack led by General Brusilov drove deep into Austrian territory, regaining much of the land lost in 1915. However, the arrival of German reinforcements saved Austria and stopped the Russian advance. Russians began to retreat into Russia. One million Russian deaths.

Key
- → Germans or their allies
- ⇒ Russians or their allies
- — The front line by 1915
- X Battle

The key events on the Eastern Front, 1914–16

The War to End Wars 1914–1919

## Why did Russia suffer so many defeats?

Despite the tremendous enthusiasm for the war in Russia, little went well and there were many crushing defeats at the hands of Germany. By the end of 1914 Russia had lost over 1 million men and by the end of 1915 Germany and Austria-Hungary had control of 13 per cent of the Russian population (16 million people). There were problems within Russia and problems at the front with the army. The table on page 62 indicates the difficulties that Russia faced at this time.

**Source A** Russian troops retreating from the Battle of Tannenberg, August 1914

**Source B** Photograph of Tsar Nicholas II blessing troops, 1915. He is holding an icon (holy picture)

**Source C** A newspaper picture of Russian gunners celebrating Brusilov's breakthrough on the South-Western front, 1916

### Tasks

1. Look at the map. In no more than 100 words, write an article for a Russian newspaper showing how the war had been disastrous for Russia.

2. What can you learn from Source B about the Russian army in 1915? (Remember how to answer this type of question? For further guidance, see page 18.)

3. How useful are Sources A and C as evidence of the preparedness of the Russian army in the First World War? (Remember how to answer this type of question? For further guidance, see pages 42 and 50.)

The defeat of Germany, 1917–18

## Reasons for Russia's defeats

| Military problems | Economic problems | Transport problems | Leadership problems |
|---|---|---|---|
| • Generals were over-confident and often incompetent.<br>• The Germans had broken the code that the Russian military used to send messages.<br>• Some generals felt that the use of cavalry would enable them to win the war. | • Russia's economy was still very dependent on farming rather than manufacturing and heavy industry.<br>• It had insufficient steelworks, shipyards and munitions factories to supply its armed forces properly. | • Supplies became bogged down on Russia's dreadful roads.<br>• The railway system was inadequate for moving supplies and troops.<br>• The telegraph system was outdated. | • The Tsar was a poor military commander.<br>• Peasants lost faith in the Tsar.<br>• The Tsar was blamed for defeats. |

### Tasks

**4.** Examine the table that shows the reasons for Russia's defeats in the years 1914–16.

a) After class discussion about the reason for the defeat of Russia, rank the reasons in order of importance in the defeats that Russia experienced.

b) Which do you think was the most important reason for the defeats? Explain your answer.

## The impact of the defeats on Russia

Eventually the military defeats led to tremendous social, economic and political problems for Russia. There was massive **inflation** and severe food shortages. On top of this, industry began to suffer, making it difficult for Russia to sustain the war effort. Tsar Nicholas II had taken charge of Russian forces at the front and had left his wife to run the country in his absence. She was assisted by Rasputin, a holy man with alleged magical powers. Defeats and incompetent government meant that support for Nicholas and his wife ebbed away very quickly. By the end of 1916, many Russian soldiers on the Eastern Front began to **desert**.

The situation worsened for Nicholas in early 1917. The number of strikes increased and the army mutinied in the capital, Petrograd. Nicholas was no longer in control and he **abdicated** in February 1917. This was the February Revolution.

**Source D** A photograph showing Russian deserters, including officers, in December 1916

**Source E** From a letter written by Lenin, the leader of the Bolsheviks, who wanted to overthrow the Tsarist government. It was written in December 1916

*A total absence of patriotic feeling can be seen in the mood of the working masses. The high cost of living, exploitation, and the barbaric policy of the government has proved to the masses the true nature of the war. There is an increase in strikes throughout the country. Prices have gone up five to ten times compared to last year. Clothing and footwear are becoming unobtainable and you no longer talk about meat.*

The War to End Wars 1914–1919

**Source F** A photograph showing people queuing for bread in Petrograd in early 1917

The new government in Russia continued the war but there was little popular support for it. It was plagued by internal political trouble, too, and a further revolution took place in October, headed by Vladimir Lenin, the leader of the Bolsheviks. Lenin and the Bolsheviks had promised the Russian people 'Peace, land and bread' and accordingly signed an **armistice** with Germany in November 1917. A peace treaty between Russia and Germany was agreed at Brest-Litovsk in March 1918.

The end of hostilities with Russia meant that Germany was now able to move troops to the Western Front. There was a degree of urgency for Germany because it was keen to launch an attack against Britain and France before large numbers of US forces arrived in Europe (see pages 66–67).

**Source G** From the report of General Alekseev to the Russian Minister of War in April 1917

*The situation grows worse every day. Information coming in from all sides indicates that our army is falling apart.*

1. *Desertions continue all the time . . .*
2. *Discipline declines with each passing day . . .*
3. *The authority of officers and commanders has collapsed and cannot be restored . . . the morale of the officers has sunk to a new low.*
4. *A mood for peace has developed in the ranks.*
5. *Anti-war propaganda is circulating in the army.*

## Tasks

5. Does Source G support Source D about the impact of the defeats on the Russian army? (Remember how to answer this type of question? For further guidance, see pages 30–31.)

6. What can you learn from Source F about the impact of the war on Russia? (Remember how to answer this type of question? For further guidance, see page 18.)

7. How useful are Sources E and G as evidence of the situation in Russia in 1916 and 1917? (Remember how to answer this type of question? For further guidance, see pages 42 and 50.)

The defeat of Germany, 1917–18

# Why and with what effect did the USA enter the war in 1917?

**Source A** Photograph of a US supply train in Northern France, 1918

**Source B** A cartoon published in 1917 showing a British view of the USA's neutrality

## Tasks

1. What can you learn from Source A about the American entry into the First World War? (Remember how to answer this type of question? For further guidance, see page 18.)

2. What can you learn from Source B about British attitudes to the USA in 1917? (Remember how to answer this type of question? For further guidance, see page 18.)

The War to End Wars 1914–1919

**Source C** An illustration of the sinking of the *Lusitania*, published in *The Graphic*, 1915

**Source D** A cartoon published in an American magazine, 1915

"CAWNT YOU SEE 'IM A BLOOMING YANKEE!"

WHO ISS IT, VAT BOAT?

LUSITANIA

JOHN BULL USES THE AMERICAN FLAG FOR PROTECTION
From the *American* (New York)

The USA remained neutral in the war until April 1917 and then entered on the side of the Allies. They had almost entered in 1915 when Germany had introduced the policy of unrestricted submarine warfare. There had been a tremendous outcry in the USA in May 1915 when the British passenger liner *Lusitania* was sunk with the loss of 1198 lives, including 128 Americans (see page 53). Germany justified the attack by saying that the *Lusitania* was carrying munitions and was therefore a legitimate target. President Wilson demanded **reparations** and an assurance that such an attack would not recur. As a result of the US reaction, Germany cut back its attacks on merchant shipping and ended unrestricted submarine warfare, which ensured the USA's continued neutrality. However, the death of so many US citizens and then the sinking of US vessels led to a deterioration of relations between Germany and the USA.

In 1917, when German submarines began attacking neutral vessels that were heading for British ports, Wilson warned that the USA would take any steps necessary if US citizens were killed or ships sunk. In February, Germany reintroduced unrestricted submarine warfare; President Wilson asked the German government to reconsider. US ships refused to sail to Britain and tons of goods piled up at docks across the country. Wilson broke off relations with Germany.

### Tasks

3. How useful are Sources C and D as evidence of the sinking of the Lusitania? (Remember how to answer this type of question? For further guidance see pages 42 and 50.)

4. Write a brief article for a German newspaper about the sinking of the *Lusitania*.

5. What is meant by the term 'unrestricted submarine warfare'?

The defeat of Germany, 1917–18

## The Zimmermann Telegram

As the argument about submarine warfare broke out in early 1917, Britain gave the US government a translation of a coded message that it had intercepted. Sent from the German Foreign Minister, Zimmermann, to the German ambassador in Mexico, the message was to the effect that if the USA entered the war, then Mexico should ally itself with Germany. Germany was proposing to give financial aid to Mexico and, following a German victory, would return to Mexico its former territories of Texas, Arizona and New Mexico, which were by then part of the USA. Germany was also hoping to create some form of agreement with Japan. If successful, these friendships would divert the USA's attention from the European war zone. Neither attempt to form an alliance was successful. The Zimmermann telegram served only to push the USA closer towards the Allies.

**Source E** A US cartoon commenting on the Zimmermann Telegram, 1917. The cartoon shows the Kaiser making a promise to a Mexican peasant

*SOME PROMISE!*

### Task

6. What can you learn from Source E about US attitudes to Germany in 1917? (Remember how to answer this type of question? For further guidance, see page 18.)

## The US declaration of war

Relations between the USA and Germany further worsened in March 1917 when four US ships were sunk with the loss of 36 lives. The overthrow of Russia's Tsar Nicholas II in the same month meant that Wilson and others in the US government now felt more able to join Britain and France because they would not be allying with the **autocratic government** of Russia. They could put over the idea of a war being fought for democracy against the **tyranny** of Germany and Austria-Hungary to the people of the USA.

On 6 April 1917, the USA declared war on Germany.

**Source F** From President Wilson's address to Congress (US parliament) in April 1917

*It is a fearful thing to lead this great peaceful people into war, into the most terrible and disastrous of all wars, civilisation itself seeming to be in the balance ... We shall fight for the things we have always carried nearest our hearts – for democracy, for the right of those who submit to authority to have a say in their own Governments, for the rights and liberties of small nations ...*

## US contribution

From the beginning of the USA's involvement in the war, President Wilson stressed that it was seeking to remove the tyranny of autocratic governments like that of Germany. Britain and France saw the total defeat of Germany as paramount, and France, in particular, wanted to ensure that Germany would no longer be the most powerful country in Europe. The differing aims of the Allies were to become problematic at the end of the war as they attempted to agree a peace settlement with Germany.

The War to End Wars 1914–1919

**Source G** A US film poster of 1917. Pershing was the commander of US forces in Europe

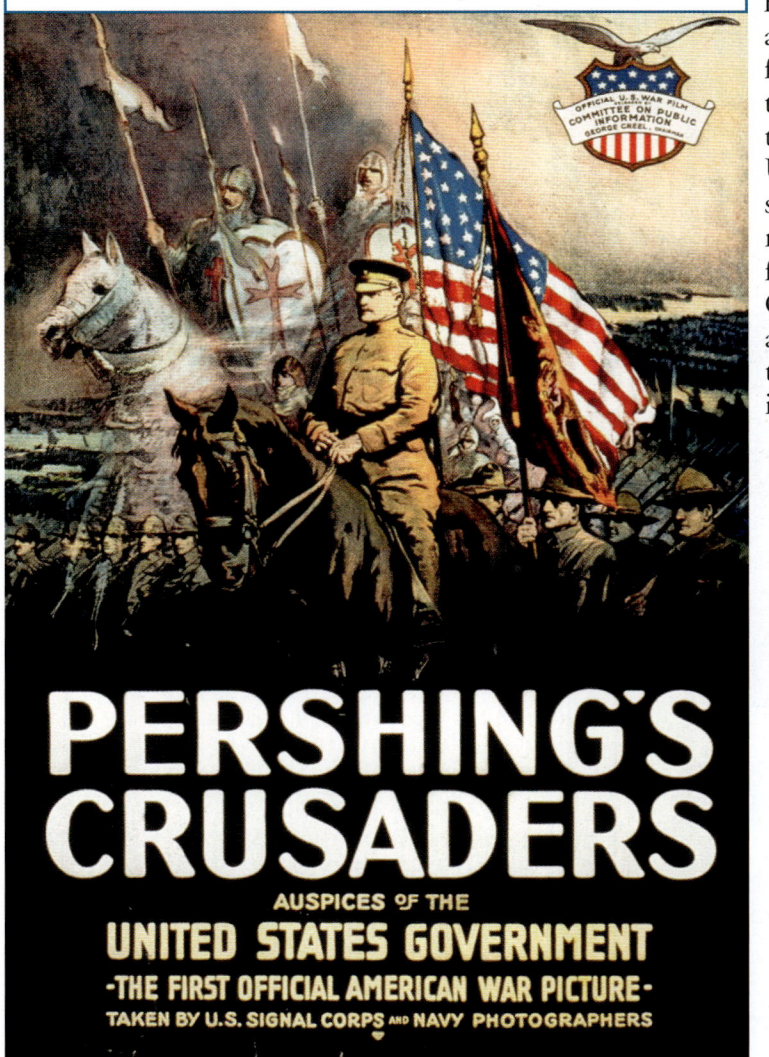

**PERSHING'S CRUSADERS**
AUSPICES OF THE
UNITED STATES GOVERNMENT
- THE FIRST OFFICIAL AMERICAN WAR PICTURE -
TAKEN BY U.S. SIGNAL CORPS AND NAVY PHOTOGRAPHERS

By the end of 1917, there were 200,000 US soldiers in Europe but they did not have the level of training that the British and French had. The arrival of the US forces was a welcome relief to the Allies on the Western Front and gave fresh impetus to the war-weary troops serving there. The US forces that arrived in 1918 had been subjected to more rigorous training and made important contributions to the fighting, helping to halt the German Spring Offensive. They were successful in two areas in the Allies' offensive in the final three months of the war – at St Mihiel and in the Meuse-Argonne.

**Source H** Table showing numbers of US forces in the First World War

|  | Numbers of US forces (men & women) |
|---|---|
| Mobilised | 4,355,000 |
| Active service on Western Front | 1,950,000 |
| Killed in action | 36,931 |
| Died of wounds | 13,673 |
| Died of disease (mainly influenza) | 62,668 |
| Deaths from other causes | 6,872 |
| Total dead | 120,144 |
| Total wounded | 198,059 |
| Total casualties | 318,203 |

### Tasks

**7.** How useful are Sources F and G as evidence of the reasons why the USA entered the First World War? (Remember how to answer this type of question? For further guidance, see pages 42 and 50.)

**8.** Working in pairs, list the reasons why the USA declared war on Germany. Place the reasons in order of importance and explain your choice.

**9.** What can you learn about US involvement in the First World War from the statistics in Source H? (Remember how to answer this type of question? For further guidance, see page 18.)

# What was the Spring Offensive and why did it fail?

**Source A** Photograph of German troops advancing through St Quentin, March 1918

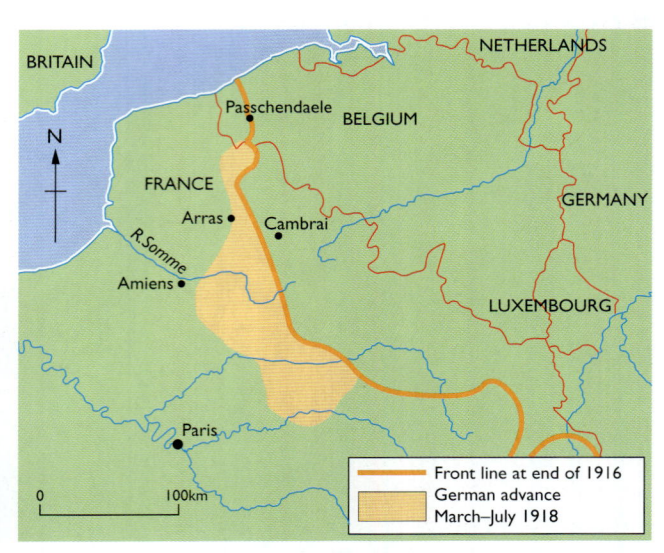

Map showing the Western Front and the extent of the German advance by July 1918

## Task

1. What can you learn from Source A about the German attack in 1918? (Remember how to answer this type of question? For further guidance, see page 18.)

By the end of 1917, Germany's army **High Command** was aware that the longer the war went on, the less likely Germany was to win. US troops had arrived on the Western Front and, at the Battle of Cambrai, British tanks and infantry had broken through German lines. Moreover, the Allied blockade was affecting food supplies, not only to the German people but also to the army. There had to be prompt action.

General Ludendorff and Field Marshal Hindenburg decided on a dramatic attempt to win the war. The cessation of hostilities with Russia meant that Germany had been able to transfer more than 500,000 troops to the Western Front. It was hoped that these troops would be able to defeat the exhausted British, who had made several attacks in the latter part of 1917.

### Biography Erich Ludendorff (1865–1937)

- 1883 Commissioned in the German army
- 1894 Joined the army General Staff
- 1904–13 Chief of mobilisation section. Key tasks included ensuring the effectiveness of the Schlieffen Plan (see pages 10–11)
- 1914 Helped plan the German victories at Tannenberg and Masurian Lakes (see page 60)
- 1916 Deputy Chief of Staff under Hindenburg. However, Ludendorff was essentially the man running Germany
- 1918 Planned Operation Michael

Ludendorff's aim was to cut through the Somme and then wheel north-west to cut the British lines of communication. He intended to avoid the British strong points and sweep behind the British forces in order to cut them off from the French. The offensive was codenamed Operation Michael.

The Germans opened their attack on 21 March 1918, using artillery and mustard gas. They advanced eight kilometres on the first day and the British soldiers retreated in chaos. The German forces moved towards Paris and got to within 60 kilometres of the capital.

The Germans had moved quickly – too quickly. The supporting forces, bringing essential supplies of munitions and food as well as fresh troops, could not keep up with the advance. One key point that led to the failure of the attack was the time German soldiers spent **looting** French shops in the areas they captured. Some seized food because they were hungry but others became caught up in the general looting.

By the time the offensive was drawn to a close at the end of July, the Germans had suffered 880,000 casualties. At this point, Ludendorff said he needed 200,000 fresh troops each month to continue the war, and he was told that the reserves could only provide about 300,000 for the whole of the next twelve months. The German High Command had made its gamble and now knew that defeat was not far away. The failure of Operation Michael meant that the Allies could go on the offensive.

**Biography** Paul von Hindenburg (1847–1934)

1866 Commissioned in the German army
1878 Joined the army General Staff
1905 Promoted to general
1914 Appointed commander-in-chief of armies in the east. Given the rank of field marshal. Led the German forces to victory at Tannenberg and the Masurian Lakes
1916 Chief of Staff of the German army

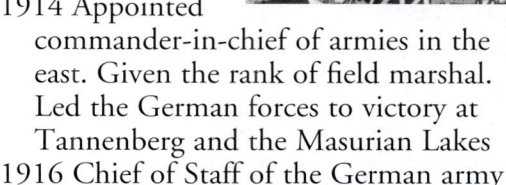

**Source B** Haig's Order of the Day, 23 March 1918. This was issued shortly after the beginning of the German offensive

> SPECIAL ORDER OF THE DAY
> By FIELD-MARSHAL SIR DOUGLAS HAIG
> K.T., G.C.B., G.C.V.O., K.C.I.E
> Commander-in-Chief, British Armies in France.
>
> To ALL RANKS OF THE BRITISH ARMY IN FRANCE AND FLANDERS.
>
> We are again at a crisis in the War. The enemy has collected on this front every available Division, and is aiming at the destruction of the British Army. We have already inflicted on the enemy in the course of the last two days very heavy loss, and the French are sending troops as quickly as possible to our support. I feel that everyone in the Army, fully realising how much depends on the exertions and steadfastness of each one of us, will do his utmost to prevent the enemy from attaining his object.
>
> General Headquarters,
> 23rd March, 1918.
>
> D. Haig. F.M.
> Commander-in-Chief,
> British Armies in France.

## Tasks

**2.** Explain why Operation Michael failed.

**3.** Study Source B. How does Haig put over his message about the seriousness of the situation as a result of the German offensive?

# How and why did Germany collapse in 1918?

When the surrender of Germany came in November 1918, it did so rather unexpectedly. The surrender had its roots not only in the failure of Operation Michael but also in the longer-term issue of the blockade imposed by the British navy. Furthermore, by the summer of 1918, the intervention of the USA had become quite significant. It was ironic that just at the time when Britain and France were being helped by a new ally, Germany's own allies were disintegrating. Bulgaria, Austria-Hungary and Turkey had suffered defeats and were seeking ceasefires.

**Source A** From a book on the history of the modern world

*By 1918 Ludendorff was growing short of the means of waging war – essential supplies of rubber, oil and food. The great German war machine was giving way under the constant strain of four years of fighting. Germany could not go on much longer.*

**Source B** A queue for potatoes in Berlin, late 1917

The War to End Wars 1914–1919

**Source C** Crowds gather around a soup distributor in Berlin, 1918

**Source D** A member of the German government speaking to a colleague in October 1918

*We have no meat. Potatoes cannot be delivered because we are short of trucks. We need 4000 trucks a day. Fat is unobtainable. The shortage is so great it is a mystery to me what the people of Berlin live on.*

## Tasks

1. Does Source B support the evidence of Sources A and C about the effects of the British naval blockade of Germany? (Remember how to answer this type of question? For further guidance, see pages 30–31.)

2. Explain why the British naval blockade was important in the war.

3. How useful is Source D as evidence of the impact of the naval blockade on Germany? (Remember how to answer this type of question? For further guidance, see pages 42 and 50.)

The British navy blockaded German ports from early 1915, and the effects were soon seen on the German people and the war effort. By the end of the second year of the war, **imports** had fallen by almost half on 1913 levels, and agriculture was severely hit by the inability to import fertilisers. With most of Germany's ships trapped in its own ports, the import of iron ore from Sweden was ended. This meant that Germany had to rely on seizing materials from the countries it had conquered.

By the winter of 1917, the supply of potatoes had run out and the only real alternative was turnips. This is why the winter of 1916–17 is known as the 'Turnip Winter'. The outbreak of influenza in October 1917 added to the discontent that was growing inside Germany. The civilians held on, but the constant queuing for food was eroding enthusiasm for the war.

At the beginning of 1918, there was **rationing** in Germany and the average food intake was 1000 calories. Rationing and poor diet hit civilians as well as soldiers (see page 68) and the death rate was 37 per cent higher in 1918 than it had been in 1913. Moreover, further outbreaks of influenza weakened many soldiers in the spring and summer of 1918.

The defeat of Germany, 1917–18

### The impact of the Bolshevik Revolution

The impact of the Bolshevik Revolution in Russia was also important because many **socialists** in Germany saw the chance to copy Lenin and remove the Kaiser. They saw the idea of establishing a socialist country as a real possibility, and there was an increasing number of strikes in October 1918. **Workers' councils** were set up across Germany. A **general strike** was proclaimed for 9 November in Berlin. It seemed that a revolution was at hand.

> **Source E** From *My War Memoirs* by Erich Ludendorff, written in 1919 when he was in exile in Sweden
>
> 8 August was the blackest day of the German army in the history of the war. This was the worst experience I had to go through. Our losses reached such proportions that we had to disband a series of divisions. 8 August made things clear for both army commands.

### The military collapse of Germany

The failure of Operation Michael was the sign to the German High Command that they could not win the war. The counter-attack to Operation Michael was launched on 8 August 1918 and saw an integrated approach from the Allies. There was an artillery bombardment and then an aerial attack, which was followed by infantry and 456 tanks. The Germans gave up land they had won following Operation Michael and were then forced to retreat beyond the Hindenburg Line, the defensive trench system they had created in 1917. It was extremely well fortified with **pillboxes** and concrete dug-outs. On the day of the counter-attack, the German army began to retreat on a 320-kilometre front with 27,000 soldiers killed and 15,000 taken prisoner.

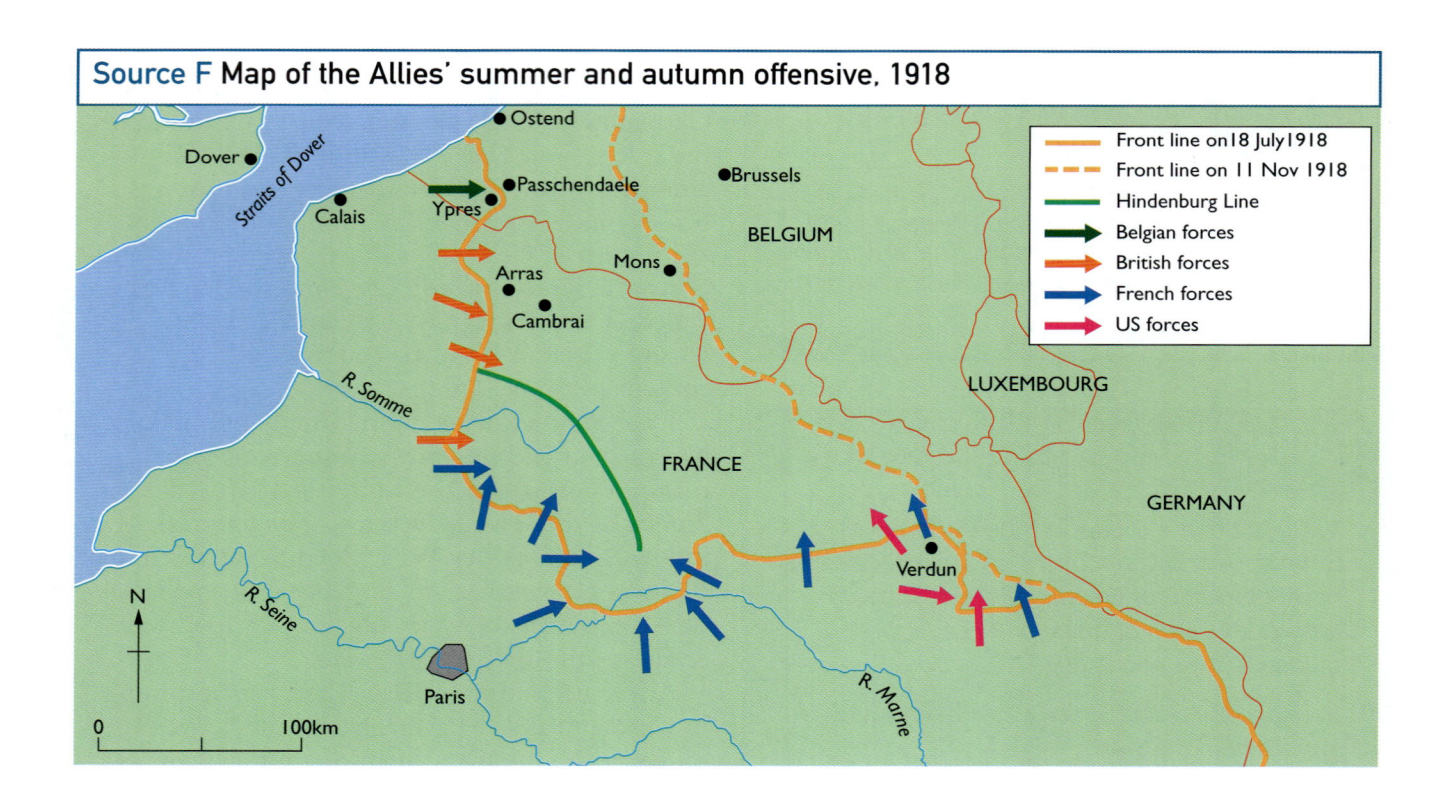

**Source F** Map of the Allies' summer and autumn offensive, 1918

*The War to End Wars 1914–1919*

By the end of September, Germany's allies were crumbling. Austria-Hungary was exhausted and Turkey was seeking an armistice. On 28 September, Bulgaria surrendered and within the next five days Austria-Hungary and Turkey signed armistices. The prospect of huge amounts of supplies pouring in from the USA now convinced Ludendorff and Hindenburg that the war was lost.

### Tasks

**4.** How useful is Source E as evidence about the impact on the German army of the Allies' counter-attack of 8 August 1918? (Remember how to answer this type of question? For further guidance, see pages 42 and 50.)

**5.** What can you learn from Source F about the Allies' counter-attack of 1918? (Remember how to answer this type of question? For further guidance, see page 18.)

## The Kiel Mutiny

At the end of October, German sailors at Kiel mutinied and refused to accept the order to put to sea. The German admirals planned to attack the British navy but there was little support among the sailors for such a plan. The army was not sent to crush this mutiny because the government could not be confident that the soldiers would not join the sailors in their revolt.

## The armistice

Chaos continued in Germany, and the government collapsed on 9 November. Kaiser Wilhelm II abdicated and fled to the Netherlands. The new government of the **Social Democratic Party** concluded an armistice with the Allies on 11 November 1918. Germany had been defeated, and the vast majority of its citizens had been aware for only a few weeks that the war could not be won. There was immediate resentment. Germans blamed the politicians for the surrender, not the army.

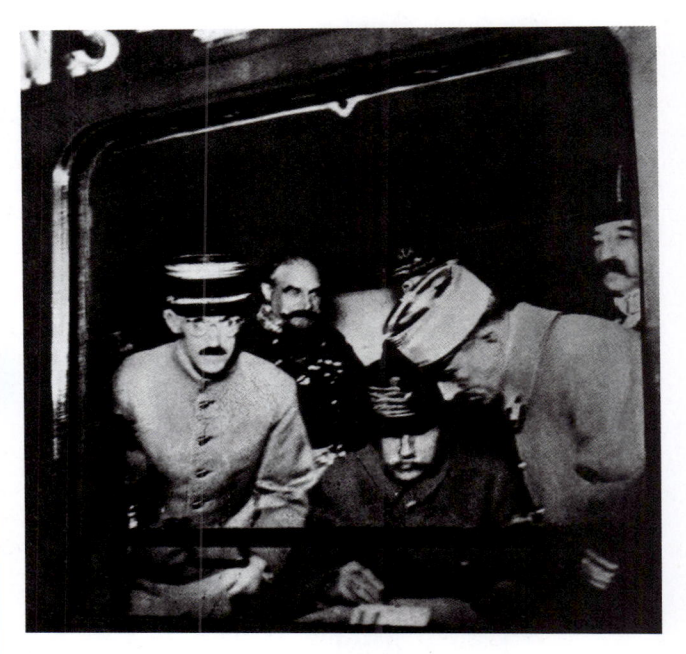

Signing of the Armistice in 1918 aboard a train

**Source G** The German government's request for an armistice, 4 October 1918

*The German government requests the President of the United States of America to take steps for the restoration of peace ... The German government accepts as a basis for peace negotiations the programme laid down by the President of the United States ...*

### Tasks

**6.** Complete the acrostic of the word 'COLLAPSE' showing the reasons why Germany collapsed in the autumn of 1918. There are a couple of examples given to help you. You need to look back over pages 68–73.

C
O
L
L
**A**merican troops arrived
P
S
**E**nthusiasm among civilians for the war declined

**7.** Read Source G. Can you suggest reasons why the Germans asked the USA to establish peace, rather than Britain and France?

The defeat of Germany, 1917–18

# Examination practice

**Source A** From a letter describing life in Berlin, written by a housewife in January 1918

*One of the most terrible of our many sufferings was having to sit in the dark. It became dark at four in the winter. It was not light until eight. Even the children could not sleep all that time ... And when they had gone to bed we were left shivering with the chill that comes from semi-starvation and which no additional clothing seems to relieve.*

**Source B** Photograph of a street kitchen in Cologne, 1918

**Source C** From a pamphlet produced in 1916 by the Spartakus League, a group of German Communists who opposed the war

*In Berlin, Leipzig, Koblenz and other German cities, starving crowds of people are rioting in front of shops for foodstuffs. In the face of these starving cries of the masses, the government is sending in more police and military patrols.*

**Source D** Poster published in the *New York Herald*, May 1917. The poster shows a German soldier, wearing pirate skull-and-crossbones and brandishing a bloody sword as he wades in a tide of women's and children's bodies

**Source E** Photograph of US troops going into action on 26 September 1918, using French tanks

**Source F** From comments made by Field Marshal Hindenburg several days after the armistice of November 1918 had been signed

*In spite of the superiority of the enemy in men and materials, we could have brought the struggle to a favourable conclusion if there had been proper co-operation between the politicians and the army. The German army was stabbed in the back.*

In question 4 on Paper 2 you are asked to explain an interpretation using:

- six sources
- your own knowledge.

This is known as the synthesis question and is worth the most marks (12). The examiner would expect you to write a minimum of one side of A4. Here is a mark scheme for the synthesis question:

| Level | Descriptor | Marks |
|---|---|---|
| 2 | Developed explanation using the sources **or** own knowledge. Developed statements using the sources **and** own knowledge | 4–7 |
| 3 | Developed explanation agreeing and/or disagreeing with the interpretation using most of the sources **and** own knowledge | 8–10 |
| 4 | A sustained argument making a balanced judgement using most of the sources **and** own knowledge. | 11–12 |

- If you only use the sources **or** your own knowledge in your answer then the maximum you can be awarded is Level 2. Use both.
- You can achieve a good Level 3 mark (8–10) by agreeing **or** disagreeing as long as you use the sources **and** your own knowledge.
- To reach Level 4 you have to give both sides **and** use the sources **and** your own knowledge **and** judgement.

## Question 1 – synthesis

'Germany was defeated in the First World War because of the entry of the USA into the war.'
Study Sources A–F. Use the Sources, and your own knowledge, to explain whether you agree with this view.

## Planning your answer

Make a copy of the table below and use it to help you plan your answer. Advice on how to write your answer is given on page 76.

1. First of all, study once again all the sources A–F.
   - Which sources agree with the interpretation? Why? In what ways? Give a brief explanation in the table. An example is given below.
   - Which sources disagree with the interpretation? Why? In what ways? Give a brief explanation in the table. An example is given below.

2. Now use your own knowledge of the defeat of Germany. To help, look again at pages 68–73.
   - What knowledge can you use to agree with the interpretation? Summarise this in your table. An example is given for you.
   - What knowledge can you use to disagree with the interpretation? Summarise this in your table.

3. To help prompt your own knowledge during an examination, underline any dates or facts in the sources that you could expand on in the answer. Expanding on sources will be classed as your own knowledge.

|  | Agrees with interpretation | Disagrees with interpretation |
|---|---|---|
| Source A |  |  |
| Source B |  |  |
| Source C |  |  |
| Source D |  |  |
| Source E | Shows US troops going into action against the Germans in 1918. |  |
| Source F |  | The German army was 'stabbed in the back'. |
| Own knowledge | By late 1918, there were almost two million US soldiers fighting in Europe. |  |

## Writing your answer

The diagram below shows the steps you should take to write a good synthesis answer. Use the steps and examples to complete the answer to question 1 on page 75.

**STEP 1**
Write an introduction that identifies the key issues you need to cover in your answer and your main argument.

*Example:*
There are a number of reasons why Germany was defeated and the entry of the USA into the war is the most important. However, other reasons such as the blockade imposed by the British navy had very serious consequences on the German war effort. Furthermore, the blockade impaired the German army's Operation Michael, which was the last push by Ludendorff and Hindenburg.

**STEP 2**
After your introduction, write a paragraph agreeing with the interpretation. Begin each paragraph with a sentence that focuses on the question, followed by your own knowledge. Use at least one of the sources to back up your own knowledge. You need to write several sentences in this paragraph.

*Example:*
The entry of the USA into the war was crucial because by late 1918, there were almost two million additional soldiers fighting the tired German army. Source E supports the interpretation because it shows US soldiers going into action in late September, the time when Germany was in retreat.

**STEP 3**
See if you can write another paragraph agreeing with the interpretation, using your own knowledge and possibly a source.

*Example:*
You could explain the impact of the entry of the USA looking at Source F, by analysing the comments made by Hindenburg and the Allies' materials and men.

*Have a go yourself*

**STEP 4**
Write a good-length paragraph disagreeing with the interpretation. Begin the paragraph with a sentence that focuses on the question, followed by your own knowledge. Use at least one of the sources to back up you own knowledge.

*Example:*
However, there are other equally important reasons behind the defeat. For example, the impact of the British naval blockade was crucial. The results of the blockade are clear in Sources A and B which indicate how civilians became hungry and lost enthusiasm for the war.

**STEP 5**
See if you can write another paragraph disagreeing with the interpretation, using your own knowledge and possibly a source.

*Example:*
You could explain the riots in some of the main German cities as shown in Source C.

*Have a go yourself*

**STEP 6**
Write a conclusion giving your final judgement on the interpretation. Do you mainly agree or disagree? Explain your judgement.

*Example:*
For the most part I agree with the interpretation. I believe that the entry of the USA helped to tip the balance. However, Germany's defeat was also the result of a number of other causes, which are linked – the blockade had a tremendous impact on the army and civilians. Moreover, military failure and shortage of manpower must be considered as important factors. The use of technology such as tanks must not be overlooked because in the summer of 1918 they did help the Allies to break through the Hindenburg Line.

# 6 The peace settlement, 1919–20

> **Source A** From Lloyd George's memo to the Allied leaders, 25 March 1919
>
> *You may strip Germany of her colonies, reduce her armaments to a mere police force and her navy to that of a fifth-rate power ... but if she feels that she has been unjustly treated in the peace of 1919 she will find means of taking revenge on her conquerors ... if we are wise we shall offer to Germany a peace, which while just, will be preferable for all sensible men to the alternative of Bolshevism.*

> **Task**
>
> What can you learn from Source A about Lloyd George's attitude towards peacemaking with Germany in 1919? (Remember how to answer this type of question? For further guidance, see page 18.)

The armistice was signed on 11 November 1918, but the actual peace treaty with Germany – the Treaty of Versailles – was not signed until 28 June 1919. This was five years to the day after the assassination of Archduke Franz Ferdinand. The peace settlement was based on US President Wilson's **Fourteen Points** which he had put forward in January 1918. Wilson was something of an idealist and his views were often at odds with those of Clemenceau, the French leader and Lloyd George, Britain's prime minister. The treaty was a compromise that suited no one, and within twenty years Europe was embroiled in a war once again.

This chapter answers the following questions:

- What were the aims of the 'Big Three'?
- What were the main terms of the Treaty of Versailles?
- Why were many Germans opposed to the treaty?
- What were the other main peace treaties?

## Source skills
You will be given the opportunity to practise all four source questions from Paper 2.

# What were the aims of the 'Big Three'?

**Source A** From a speech during the British general election campaign by Sir Eric Geddes, an MP, December 1918

*Germany is going to pay and I personally have no doubt that we will get everything out of her that you can squeeze out of a lemon and a bit more. Not only all the gold Germany has got, but all her silver and jewels shall be handed over. All her pictures and libraries shall be sold to the Allies and the proceeds used to pay the war debt. I would strip Germany as she stripped Belgium.*

## Task

1. How useful is Source A as evidence of British attitudes to Germany in 1918? (Remember how to answer this type of question? For further guidance, see pages 42 and 50.)

**Source B** Extracts from Wilson's Fourteen Points

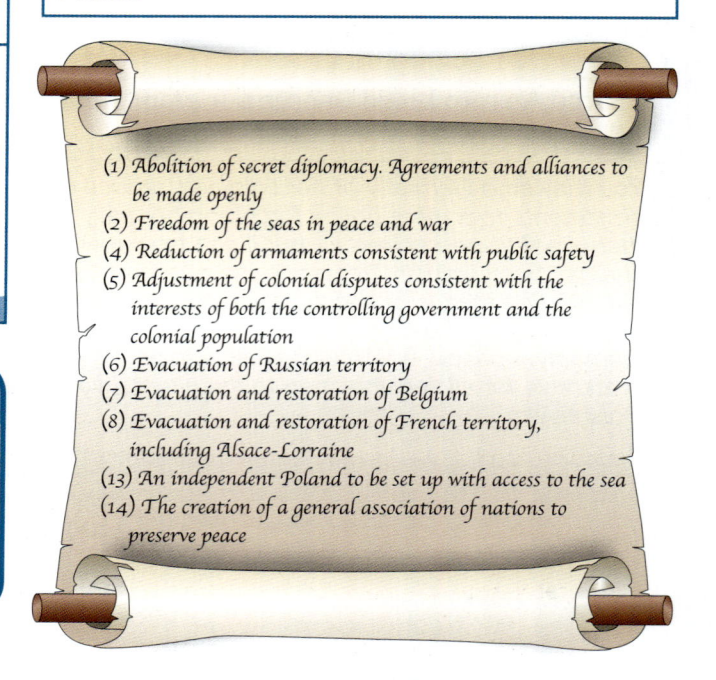

(1) Abolition of secret diplomacy. Agreements and alliances to be made openly
(2) Freedom of the seas in peace and war
(4) Reduction of armaments consistent with public safety
(5) Adjustment of colonial disputes consistent with the interests of both the controlling government and the colonial population
(6) Evacuation of Russian territory
(7) Evacuation and restoration of Belgium
(8) Evacuation and restoration of French territory, including Alsace-Lorraine
(13) An independent Poland to be set up with access to the sea
(14) The creation of a general association of nations to preserve peace

Representatives of the victorious powers met in Paris in January 1919 to discuss the fate of the defeated nations. Germany was not allowed to attend because it was immediately agreed that it had been guilty of starting the war and therefore was in no position to be granted fair treatment. Russia was not permitted to attend because its **Communist** government was seen as a threat to world stability. The Bolshevik government wished to see communist revolutions all over the world and violence was a means of achieving this. The Allies had actually sent troops to Russia to overthrow the Bolshevik government.

Despite the continued problems, President Wilson put forward some ideas that acted as a basis for the peace talks. These were known as his Fourteen Points. The first five points and the fourteenth were quite general and dealt with relations between all countries of the world. The remainder dealt with Germany and its allies. Source B shows some of the general points and those that also affected Germany.

## Task

2. Work in pairs. Copy the table below and then explain why Germany might agree or disagree with the points in Source B.

|  | Germany might agree | Germany might disagree |
|---|---|---|
| Point 1 | | |
| Point 2 | | |
| Point 4 | | |
| Point 5 | | |
| Point 6 | | |
| Point 7 | | |
| Point 8 | | |
| Point 13 | | |
| Point 14 | | |

The War to End Wars 1914–1919

The main aims of the 'Big Three' often overlapped but were sometimes at variance. Many of the discussions between them were held away from the main debating rooms in private and there were many arguments. Clemenceau once derided Wilson by saying that God had only Ten Commandments, yet Wilson had fourteen.

(From left to right) Lloyd George, Clemenceau and Wilson, at Versailles in 1919. Together, these men were known as the 'Big Three', representing the three main powers of the world.

| Post-war aims of the Big Three | | |
|---|---|---|
| **Clemenceau** | **Lloyd George** | **Wilson** |
| • Punish Germany<br>• Weaken Germany to ensure no future attacks<br>• Deprive Germany of all iron and coal resources<br>• Regain Alsace-Lorraine, taken by Germany in 1871<br>• Rebuild France using German money<br>• Create a **buffer** between France and Germany<br>• Seek reparations to cover war debts and damages<br>• Prevent the spread of Bolshevism | • Keep the British public on his side – many people wanted a severe treaty<br>• Punish Germany, but not too harshly<br>• Keep Germany as a trading partner<br>• Return Alsace-Lorraine to France<br>• Prevent the spread of Bolshevism<br>• **Self-determination** for parts of the Austro-Hungarian empire<br>• Seek reparations to cover war debts and damages<br>• Protect the British empire<br>• Protect Britain's position in international trade | • Follow his Fourteen Points, especially arms reduction<br>• A just and lasting peace for Europe<br>• Self-determination for states that had been parts of European empires before 1914<br>• Create a **League of Nations** to prevent future wars that all countries would join<br>• Make the world safe for democracy<br>• No secret treaties |

The main aims of the 'Big Three'

## Tasks

**3.** Look at the circles on the right. This is known as a Venn diagram. It is used to show how factors can overlap with each other – how issues are interlinked.

- Sketch your own Venn diagram like the one on the right.
- Use your diagram to show the overlap between the demands of Clemenceau, Lloyd George and Wilson.
- Explain what the completed Venn diagram shows.

**4.** Look at the aims of each of the Big Three. Choose three aims from each and explain why they were important to that country.

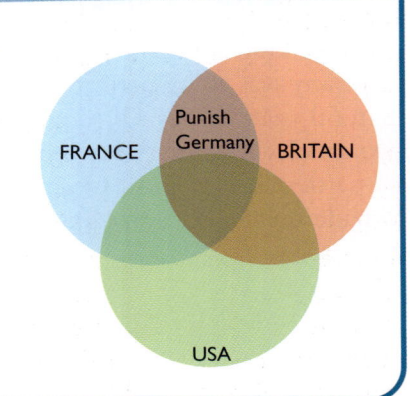

The peace settlement, 1919–20

# What were the main terms of the Treaty of Versailles?

**Source A** Article 231 from the Treaty of Versailles

*The Allied and Associated Governments affirm and Germany accepts the responsibility of Germany and her allies for causing all the loss and damage to which the Allied and Associated Governments and their nationals have been subjected as a consequence of the war imposed upon them by the aggression of Germany and her allies.*

**Source B** Article 235 from the Treaty of Versailles

*In order to enable the Allied and Associated Powers to proceed at once to the restoration of their industrial and economic life … Germany shall pay in such instalments and in such manner (whether in gold, commodities, ships, securities or otherwise) as the Reparation Commission may fix. During 1919, 1920 and the first four months of 1921, Germany will also pay the equivalent of 20,000,000,000 gold marks. Out of this sum the expenses of the armies of occupation shall first be met.*

**Source C** A cartoon published in *The Bulletin*, an Australian newspaper, on 3 July 1919, shortly after the publication of the terms of the Treaty of Versailles

"FOR THE TERM OF HIS NATURAL LIFE."

Article 231 (Source A) became known as the War Guilt Clause and it placed any blame for starting the war firmly at the feet of Germany. Moreover, having to accept the blame for the war meant that Germany had to pay reparations (Article 235 – Source B), and this figure was eventually calculated at £6.6 billion in 1921. France was able to take goods in kind until the figure was decided. Germany was to be permitted a period of more than 60 years to pay off these reparations. These two articles became the two most hated features of the settlement for most Germans. A final article forbade the unification (*Anschluss*) of Germany and Austria.

The War to End Wars 1914–1919

**Source D** A cartoon entitled 'Clemenceau the Vampire', from the German right-wing satirical magazine, *Kladderadatsch*, published in July 1919. The cartoon is commenting about the Treaty of Versailles

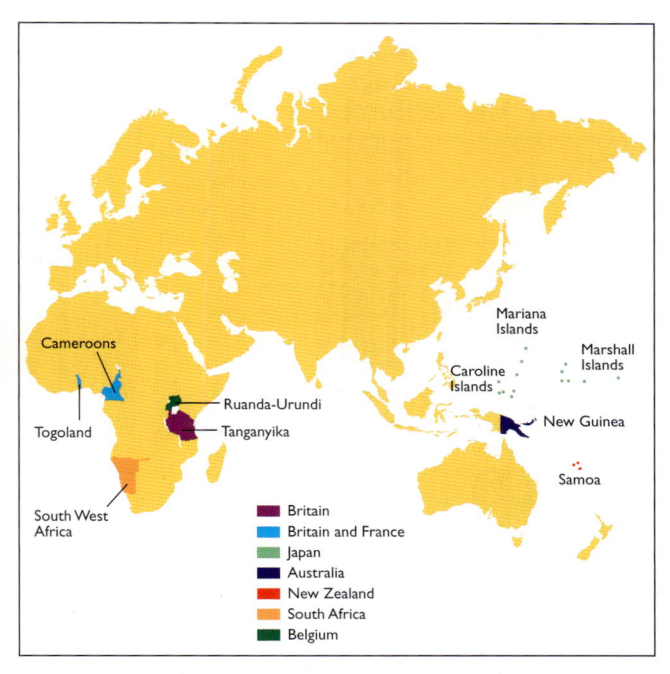

Map showing overseas territory lost by Germany at the Treaty of Versailles and the countries that were given the former German colonies as **mandated territories**

## Tasks

1. What can you learn from Sources A and B about the punishment of Germany at the Treaty of Versailles? (Remember how to answer this type of question? For further guidance, see page 18.)

2. Does Source D support the evidence of Sources B and C about the treatment of Germany in the Treaty of Versailles? (Remember how to answer this type of question? For further guidance, see pages 30–31.)

3. How useful are Sources C and D as evidence of the treatment of Germany in the Treaty of Versailles? (Remember how to answer this type of question? For further guidance, see pages 42 and 50.)

The peace settlement, 1919–20

# Germany's territorial losses

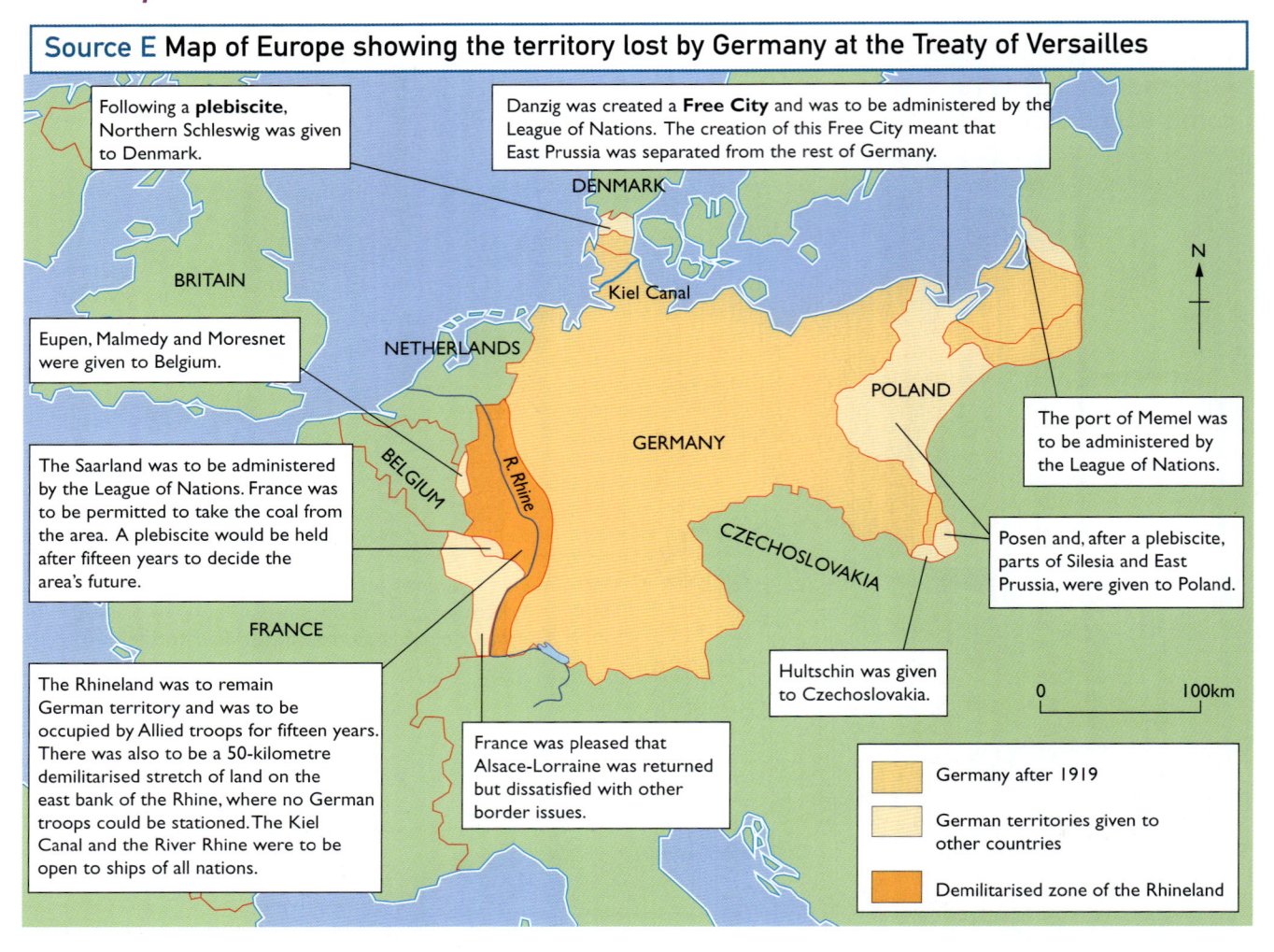

**Source E** Map of Europe showing the territory lost by Germany at the Treaty of Versailles

- Following a **plebiscite**, Northern Schleswig was given to Denmark.
- Danzig was created a **Free City** and was to be administered by the League of Nations. The creation of this Free City meant that East Prussia was separated from the rest of Germany.
- Eupen, Malmedy and Moresnet were given to Belgium.
- The Saarland was to be administered by the League of Nations. France was to be permitted to take the coal from the area. A plebiscite would be held after fifteen years to decide the area's future.
- The Rhineland was to remain German territory and was to be occupied by Allied troops for fifteen years. There was also to be a 50-kilometre demilitarised stretch of land on the east bank of the Rhine, where no German troops could be stationed. The Kiel Canal and the River Rhine were to be open to ships of all nations.
- France was pleased that Alsace-Lorraine was returned but dissatisfied with other border issues.
- The port of Memel was to be administered by the League of Nations.
- Posen and, after a plebiscite, parts of Silesia and East Prussia, were given to Poland.
- Hultschin was given to Czechoslovakia.

Legend:
- Germany after 1919
- German territories given to other countries
- Demilitarised zone of the Rhineland

## Tasks

**4.** Look at Source E and study the territorial losses of Germany. Why could France now feel secure from Germany in the future?

**5.** Write an article for a German newspaper explaining why the military terms of the Treaty of Versailles, outlined on page 83, were too severe.

**6.** How useful is Source F in helping you to understand why some Germans disliked the Treaty of Versailles? (Remember how to answer this type of question? For further guidance, see pages 42 and 50.)

The War to End Wars 1914–1919

# Military restrictions placed on Germany

## Army

- reduced to 100,000
- no conscription
- no tanks
- no heavy artillery
- no poison gas
- no German troops to be stationed in the Rhineland

## Navy

Reduced to:
- 15,000 sailors
- six battleships (no further construction of battleships)
- six light cruisers
- 12 destroyers
- 12 torpedo boats
- submarines were not permitted

## Airforce

- To be completely destroyed

**Source F** A cartoon from the German political magazine, *Simplicissimus*, June 1919. It shows Wilson, Clemenceau and Lloyd George at the guillotine with Germany

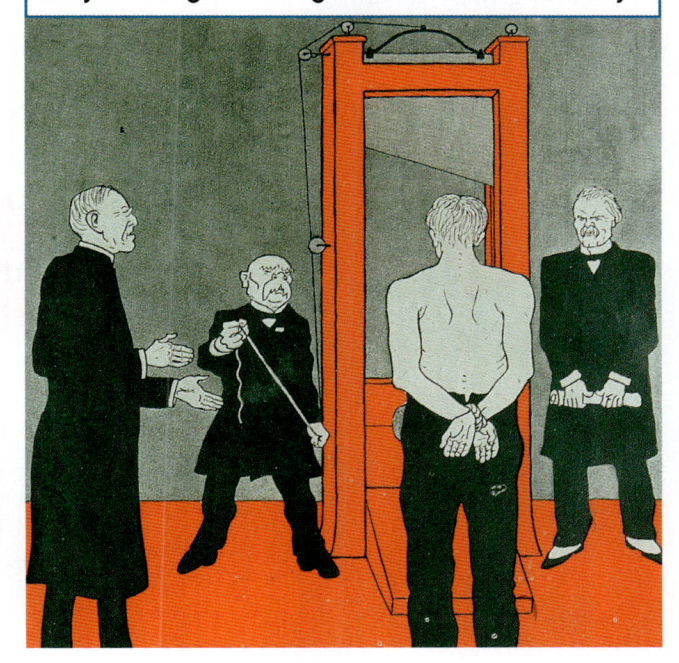

The peace settlement, 1919–20

# Why were many Germans opposed to the treaty?

**Source A** An extract from a German newspaper, *Deutsche Zeitung*, 28 June 1919

> **VENGEANCE! German nation!**
>
> Today in the Hall of Mirrors at Versailles, the disgraceful treaty is being signed. Do not forget it. The German people will with unceasing work press forward to reconquer the place among nations to which it is entitled. Then will come vengeance for the shame of 1919.

The Germans had not been invited to participate in the discussions at Versailles and were forced to accept its terms. It was called a *Diktat* in Germany – a dictated peace.

There was little that the Germans could do to retaliate. As a last defiant gesture, the German fleet was scuttled at Scapa Flow, one week before the treaty was signed. This prevented Britain from adding the German ships to its own navy.

### Tasks

1. What can you learn from Source A about German attitudes to the Treaty of Versailles? (Remember how to answer this type of question? For further guidance, see page 18.)

2. Using the concept map below to help you, in pairs, either

   a) write an article for a German newspaper explaining why you feel the Treaty of Versailles is unfair, **or**

   b) write a speech explaining why you feel the Treaty of Versailles is unfair.

   If you write the speech, try to put in lots of emotive, persuasive words – remember you are trying to inspire a crowd. For the newspaper, try to be as objective as possible.

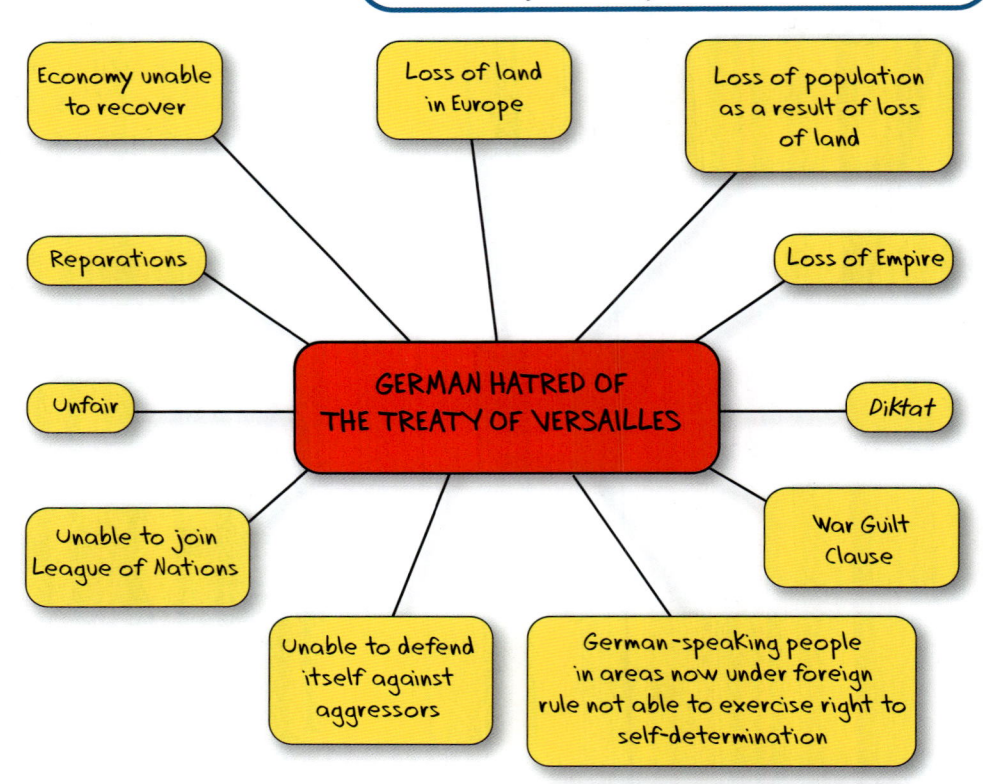

**GERMAN HATRED OF THE TREATY OF VERSAILLES**
- Economy unable to recover
- Loss of land in Europe
- Loss of population as a result of loss of land
- Reparations
- Loss of Empire
- Unfair
- Diktat
- Unable to join League of Nations
- War Guilt Clause
- Unable to defend itself against aggressors
- German-speaking people in areas now under foreign rule not able to exercise right to self-determination

A concept map of Germany's hatred for the Treaty of Versailles

The War to End Wars 1914–1919

# What were the other main peace treaties?

As well as the Treaty of Versailles, separate agreements were made with each of Germany's allies. The treaties of St. Germain (1919), Neuilly (1919) and Trianon (1920) dealt with Austria, Bulgaria and Hungary respectively. The Treaty of Sèvres (1920) dealt with Turkey and was revised in 1923 at Lausanne.

**1 The Treaty of St Germain with Austria**
10 September 1919

**Land:** Austria lost land to Czechoslovakia, Italy and Serbia (Yugoslavia)
**Army:** Reduced to 30,000 men
**Anschluss:** Union with Germany was forbidden
**Reparations:** Austria was to pay reparations but went bankrupt before the rate could be set

**2 The Treaty of Neuilly with Bulgaria**
27 November 1919

**Land:** Bulgaria lost land to Greece, Romania and Serbia (Yugoslavia)
**Army:** Reduced to 20,000 men
**Reparations:** Bulgaria had to pay £90 million in reparations

**3 The Treaty of Trianon with Hungary**
4 June 1920

**Land:** Hungary lost land to Austria, Czechoslovakia, Romania and Serbia (Yugoslavia) reducing its size from 283,000 sq km to less than 93,000 sq km. Its population was reduced from 18.2 million to 7.6 million
**Army:** Reduced to 35,000 men
**Reparations:** Hungary was to pay reparations but the amount was never set

**4 The Treaty of Sèvres with Turkey**
20 August 1920

**Land:** Turkey lost Eastern Thrace and Smyrna to Greece. The League of Nations took control of Turkey's colonies.

**The Treaty of Lausanne, 1923**
Smyrna was returned to Turkey. Turkey gave up its claims to land in the Middle East

Map legend:
- Territory lost by Austria-Hungary
- Territory lost by Bulgaria
- Territory lost by Turkey

The peace settlement, 1919–20

# Examination practice

Here is your opportunity to practise all four source questions.

**Source A** From Lloyd George's memo to the Allied leaders, 25 March 1919

*If we are wise we shall offer to Germany a peace, which while just, will be preferable for all sensible men to the alternative of Bolshevism.*

**Source B** A cartoon published by the *Daily Mirror* on 24 June 1919. Germany is represented as a schoolboy refusing to sign the Treaty of Versailles. He is being watched by his teacher – Dr Allies who makes him sign it

**Source C** From a speech by Clemenceau at Versailles, 16 June 1919

*Justice is what Germany shall have. But it must be justice for all. There must be justice for the dead and wounded and for those who have been orphaned and bereaved that Europe might be freed from German despotism. There must be justice for the peoples who now stagger under war debts which exceed £30,000,000,000. There must be justice for those millions whose homes and land, ships and property German savagery has plundered and destroyed.*

**Source D** A photograph of German tanks being broken up in Berlin, 1919

**Source E** A drawing published in the German magazine *Simplicissimus*, 27 May 1919. It illustrates that the harsh terms of the Treaty of Versailles mean there is no more sun for Germany

**Source F** From the speech made by Count Rantzau, the head of the German delegation at Versailles

*The demand is made that we shall acknowledge that Germany alone is guilty of having caused the war. Such a confession would be a lie. We deny that the people of Germany, who were convinced that they were waging a war of defence, should be burdened with the sole guilt of that war.*

## Tasks

**1.** Study Source A.
What can you learn from Source A about the Allies' attitude to Germany at Versailles?

(4 marks)

(Remember how to answer this type of question? For further guidance, see page 18.)

**2.** Study Sources A, B and C.
Does Source C support the evidence of Sources A and B about the attitude of the Allies at Versailles? Explain your answer.

(6 marks)

(Remember how to answer this type of question? For further guidance, see pages 30–31.)

**3.** Study Sources D and E.
How useful are these two sources as evidence of Germany's punishment following the Treaty of Versailles?

(8 marks)

(Remember how to answer this type of question? For further guidance, see pages 42 and 50.)

**4.** Study all the Sources.
'Disarmament was the most hated of the clauses of the Treaty of Versailles in Germany.'
Use the sources and your own knowledge to explain whether you agree with this view.

(12 marks)

(Remember how to answer this type of question? For further guidance, see pages 74–76.)

(Total 30 marks)

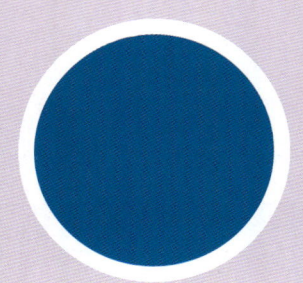

# Revision activities

## Chapter 1

1. Are the following statements true or false? If the statements are false, correct them so they are true.

   |  | True | False |
   |---|---|---|
   | a) Austria was a member of the Triple Entente |  |  |
   | b) Germany declared war on Russia on 1 August 1914 |  |  |
   | c) Britain was a member of the Triple Entente |  |  |
   | d) In 1908 Austria annexed Serbia |  |  |
   | e) There was naval rivalry between Britain and Austria |  |  |
   | f) France wanted to recover the provinces of Alsace-Lorraine |  |  |

2. Briefly explain why each of the following increased rivalry between the Great Powers:
   - Bosnia
   - the *Dreadnought*
   - Morocco
   - Alsace-Lorraine.

3. Explain why the following battles were important in 1914:
   - Mons
   - Marne
   - First Battle of Ypres.

4. Here is a block diagram of countries representing Germany, Belgium, Russia, France and Britain.

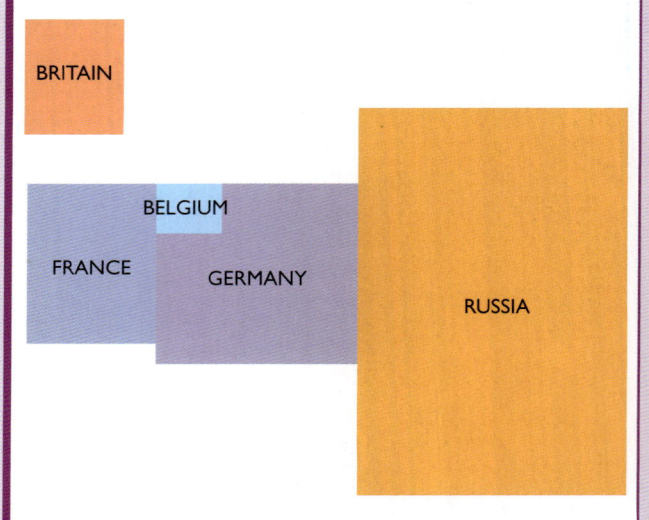

   - Make a copy and use it to show the various stages of the Schlieffen Plan.
   - Use a similar block diagram to show the reasons for the failure of the plan.

5. Which of the following statements best explain the failure of the Schlieffen Plan? Explain your choice.
   - It failed because the original plan was too ambitious.
   - It failed because von Moltke changed the original plan.
   - It failed because of the actions of the BEF.

The War to End Wars 1914–1919

6. Place the following events of 1914 in chronological order:
   - the First Battle of Ypres
   - the Battle of Le Cateau
   - the German invasion of Belgium
   - the German retreat to the Aisne
   - the British declaration of war on Germany
   - the murder at Sarajevo
   - the Austrian declaration of war on Serbia
   - the Battle of the Marne.

**Source A** A letter from a young German called up to the army in 1914 and about to leave for the front

*Such enthusiasm! The whole battalion with tunics and helmets decked with flowers. Handkerchiefs waving untiringly. Cheers on every side. Over and over again the fresh and wonderful reassurance of the soldiers.*

7. Look at Source A. Which of the following are inferences?
   - There was great enthusiasm for the war in Germany.
   - Handkerchiefs were waving untiringly and there were cheers on every side.
   - Many young Germans were keen on the war and fighting for their country.
   - Our tunics and helmets were full of flowers.

# Chapter 2

1. Match the following causes and effects about conditions on the Western Front.

| Causes | Effects |
| --- | --- |
| a) The trenches were frequently flooded. | i) The Germans knew that there was going to be an offensive on the Somme. |
| b) The British bombarded the German trenches for several days at the end of June 1916. | ii) Britain suffered nearly 60,000 casualties. |
| c) It rained throughout August 1917 in the Ypres area. | iii) Many men suffered from trench foot. |
| d) The British troops were told to walk slowly across no man's land on 1 July 1916. | iv) The battlefield became a quagmire. |

2. Categorise the importance of the following reasons for the stalemate on the Western Front, beginning with the most important in the centre to the least important on the outside:
   - the commanders
   - the machine gun
   - the failure of new weapons
   - strength of the trench system.

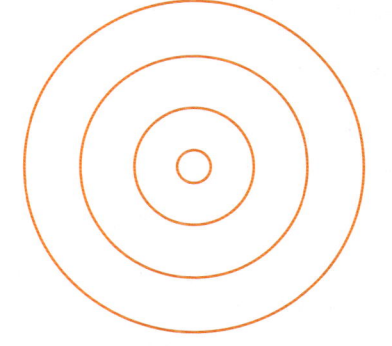

Revision activities

3. Explain the meaning of the following:
   - going over the top
   - no man's land
   - offensive
   - the front line
   - attrition
   - trench foot
   - dug-outs
   - artillery.

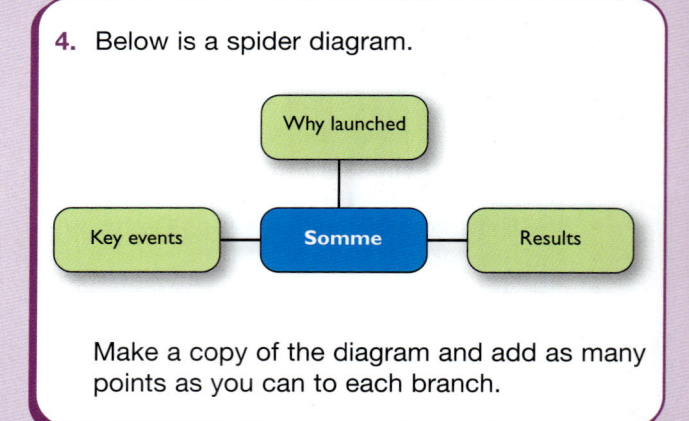

4. Below is a spider diagram.

   Why launched — Somme — Key events — Results

   Make a copy of the diagram and add as many points as you can to each branch.

5. Look again at the cross-referencing question on page 30. Now examine the following statements. Giving reasons decide which
   - you would use in your answer
   - you would not use.

| Statement | Use/Not use? Reasons? |
|---|---|
| a) Source A supports the evidence of Source B because they both mention casualties. | |
| b) Source C supports the evidence of Source B. Source B shows examples of the casualties mentioned in Source C. | |
| c) Source A says that everything went like clockwork. Source C says that there were dead and wounded everywhere. | |
| d) Source B shows wounded soldiers. Source A says the men are in wonderful spirits. | |
| e) There is strong support between C and B as both suggest that the Somme led to heavy casualties. | |

# Chapter 3

1. Draw a spider diagram showing the reasons for the following:
   - the launching of the Gallipoli campaign
   - the failure of the Gallipoli landings
   - the terrible conditions on the beaches of Gallipoli.

2. Explain the following key features of the Battle of Jutland:
   - why all four fleets converged on Jutland at the same time
   - the importance of the cruiser battle
   - why both sides claimed victory.

The War to End Wars 1914–1919

3. Make a copy of the following table and decide how important each of the events was in the war at sea. Give a brief explanation for each decision.

|  | Decisive | Important | Unimportant |
|---|---|---|---|
| German raids on British coast |  |  |  |
| Battle of Dogger Bank |  |  |  |
| Battle of Heligoland Bight |  |  |  |
| The British blockade of Germany |  |  |  |

4. Who or what were the following:
   - the Anzacs
   - the Dardanelles
   - Admiral Scheer
   - Admiral Beatty
   - General Hamilton?

5. Look again at the second question on utility on page 42.
   - Which of the following statements would you use in your answer?
   - Which would you not use?
   
   Give reasons for your choices.

| Statement | Use/Not use? Reasons? |
|---|---|
| a) Source B says that the men rowed ashore but were dropped off 50 metres from the beach. |  |
| b) Source B is useful because it suggests that the Turks were prepared for the landings. |  |
| c) Source B is useful because it suggests that the landings failed due to lack of leadership from the officers. |  |
| d) Source B also says that once the men landed they were scared out of their wits. |  |

# Chapter 4

1. a) 'Aeroplanes were of little use in the First World War.'
   Write two or three sentences agreeing with this statement.
   b) 'Aeroplanes were of great use in the First World War.'
   Write two or three sentences agreeing with this statement.

2. Are the following statements about the First World War true or false?

|  | True | False |
|---|---|---|
| a) Gas killed more than one million soldiers in the war. |  |  |
| b) Q ships protected convoys. |  |  |
| c) Tanks were first used at the Battle of the Somme. |  |  |
| d) The British and Germans used aeroplanes to bomb civilians. |  |  |
| e) The Battle of Cambrai was the first time that tanks were used successfully. |  |  |

3. Place the following events in chronological order:
   - sinking of the Lusitania
   - first use of gas
   - introduction of tanks
   - use of the convoy system.

4. Explain, in no more than a sentence, what you know about the following:
   - the problems tanks faced in the First World War
   - the use of poison gas
   - Q ships
   - U-boats
   - the nature of a source
   - the origins of a source.

Revision activities

5. Make a copy of the following table and give at least three reasons in each column to show the advantages of each weapon.

| Tanks | Gas | U-boats |
|---|---|---|
|  |  |  |
|  |  |  |
|  |  |  |

# Chapter 5

1. The following account of events in the First World War is by a student who has not revised thoroughly. Rewrite the account, correcting any errors.

   *The USA entered the war in 1918 after the Russian Revolution of September that year. Britain was starving Germany with its U-boats and so Germany decided to have a Winter Offensive, but this failed. Then Britain and its allies had their Spring Offensive and soon defeated Germany by December 1918.*

2. Match the word to the definition:

   **Words:**
   a) abdicate
   b) Triple Entente
   c) armistice
   d) inflation
   e) mutiny

   **Definitions:**
   i) A rise in prices caused by too much money and credit relative to the available goods
   ii) A rebellion by members of the armed forces against their officers
   iii) Give up the throne
   iv) An agreement formed in 1907 between Russia, France and Britain
   v) Cessation of hostilities

3. Explain in no more than one sentence what you know about the following:
   - the Battle of Tannenberg
   - the Brusilov Offensive
   - the sinking of the *Lusitania*
   - the Zimmermann Telegram
   - Operation Michael
   - the 'Turnip Winter'
   - the Hindenburg Line.

4. There is always more than one interpretation of an event. Here are four interpretations. See whether you can add your own in the adjacent column.

| Interpretation | Your own interpretation |
|---|---|
| a) The British naval blockade was the main reason Germany was defeated. |  |
| b) German civilians were affected more by the Bolshevik Revolution than by food shortages. |  |
| c) Operation Michael failed because German soldiers were not adequately supplied. |  |
| d) Germany asked for an armistice because its allies were surrendering. |  |

# Chapter 6

1. What were the following:
   - the Big Three
   - the Fourteen Points
   - Alsace-Lorraine
   - Article 231
   - *Anschluss*
   - reparations
   - conscription?

2. Summarise in five words or fewer the terms of the Treaty of Versailles in relation to the following:

|  | **Summary of terms imposed on Germany** |
|---|---|
| Army |  |
| Navy |  |
| Air force |  |
| Empire |  |

3. The following account of the peace settlement is by a student who has not revised thoroughly. Rewrite the account, correcting any errors.

   *In the Treaty of Versailles President Lloyd George of the USA put forward his 15 Points and dealt with Germany. Clemenceau of France wanted to be soft on Germany but did want the province of Alsace-Anschluss back. Germany was found guilty of starting the war in 1915, and had to pay 600 million pounds damages, called preparations. Germany lost the Tsarland which had coal mines and could not join the United Nations.*

4. Match the word to the definition:

   **Words:**
   a) plebiscite
   b) conscription
   c) self-determination
   d) mandated territories
   e) buffer

   **Definitions:**
   i) A small and usually neutral state between two rival powers
   ii) The right of a people to decide its own form of government without influence from outside
   iii) A direct vote of the people on one specific issue
   iv) Lands taken from the Central Powers' empires to be prepared for future independence
   v) Compulsory military service

5. Was France safe from Germany as a result of the Treaty of Versailles? Make a copy of the scales below and add evidence to each side.

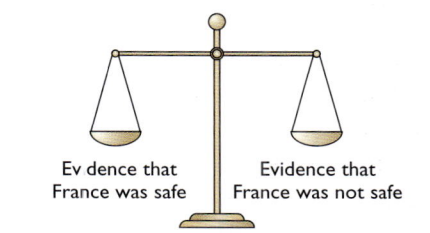

   Evidence that France was safe | Evidence that France was not safe

Revision activities

# Glossary

**abdicate**  Give up the throne
**amphibious operation**  An attack launched from the sea but using land troops
**armistice**  An agreement to stop fighting in advance of peace negotiations
**artillery**  Heavy guns
**August 1918 offensive**  The Allied counter-attack following Operation Michael
**autocratic government**  Government in which one person has absolute power

**barrage**  An attack on enemy positions using heavy guns, often preceding an attack by infantry
**blockade**  To prevent supplies from reaching their destination by sea
**Bolsheviks**  A political party that seized power from the Provisional Government of Russia in October/November 1917, with the aim of giving power to the working classes
**British Expeditionary Force (BEF)**  A small, professional army sent to support France and Belgium at the outbreak of war
**buffer**  A small and usually neutral state between two rival powers

**cavalry**  Soldiers on horseback
**ceasefire**  A period of truce when fighting is suspended
**censor**  To check letters, films, newspapers, etc. and remove any parts that might give useful information to the enemy
**Central Powers**  Austria and Germany
**cholera**  Severe digestive infection caused by contaminated food or water
**Communist**  Belief based on the ideas of Karl Marx
**conscription**  Compulsory military service
**convoy system**  Merchant vessels sailing in groups with an escort of warships

**depth charges**  Explosive devices that went off at a pre-determined depth. The resultant explosion, if near a submarine, would either destroy, cripple or cause it to surface and surrender
**desert**  To leave one's post or unit without permission
**destroyers**  Small, fast, heavily armed warships
***Dreadnought***  The most modern and powerful battleship launched before the First World War
**dug-out**  Underground shelter for soldiers (especially in trenches)
**dysentery**  A severe infection affecting the digestive system

**filter respirators**  Breathing apparatus that protected soldiers from inhaling poisonous gases
**First Lord of the Admiralty**  Member of the government responsible for the navy
**fleet**  A number of ships grouped together
**Fourteen Points**  Principles laid down by President Wilson as the war aims of the USA
**Free City**  A city declared to be independent of any national government, guaranteed by the League of Nations

**general strike**  A strike by most or all of the workers of a country, province, city, etc.

**High Command**  The commander-in-chief and senior officers of a nation's armed forces

**imports**  The purchase of goods or services from foreign countries
**inflation**  A rise in prices caused by too much money and credit relative to the available goods

**Kaiser**  German emperor

**League of Nations**  The international body founded in 1920 with the aim of preserving world peace; its establishment was the last of President Wilson's Fourteen Points
**looting**  Seizing goods

**magazine**  Ammunition store
**mandated territories**  Lands taken from the Central Powers' empires and placed under the government of other countries, to be prepared for future independence
**merchant ships**  Vessels involved in commercial trading
**mines**  Devices containing explosives; sea mines were designed to blow up vessels that came into contact with them
**mobilise**  Prepare a nation's armed forces for war
**mutiny**  Open rebellion against authority; refusal to obey orders

**neutral**  Not assisting either side in a war
**no man's land**  The area between enemy lines, to which neither side lays claim

**offensive**  A major, sustained attack designed to achieve a significant military objective
**outflank**  To go round the side (flank) of the opposing army

**pillboxes**  Fortified gun positions, usually made of concrete

**plebiscite**  A direct vote of the people on one specific issue

**provenance**  The origin of a source – where it comes from and/or who produced it

**rationing**  Restricting food and other goods to a fixed allowance, to ensure adequate supplies to meet the essential needs of the population

**reconnaissance balloons**  Hot-air balloons from which observers could gather information about the enemy's position

**reparations**  Compensation demanded from a defeated nation after a war

**self-determination**  The right of a people to determine its own form of government without influence from outside

**Social Democratic Party**  German socialist party founded in 1863

**socialists**  Believers in the idea that there should be state ownership and control of the means of production, distribution and exchange

**Spring Offensive**  The German offensive that began in March 1918, also known as Operation Michael and the Ludendorff Offensive

**tear gas**  Gas that causes the eyes to water, resulting in temporary blindness

**Triple Entente**  An agreement formed in 1907 between Russia, France and Britain, also known as the Allies

**typhoid**  A disease characterised by a high temperature and stomach pains

**tyranny**  A government that is oppressive and unjust

**U-boats**  German submarines

**ultimatum**  A final demand

**war of attrition**  A war in which the opponents try to wear each other down

**workers' councils**  Councils set up by workers to control their workplace

# Index

aeroplanes 43, 56–7
Alekseev, General 63
Alliance system 8
Alsace-Lorraine 8, 10, 13
ANZACs (Australian and New Zealand Army Corps) 38, 40
armistice 73, 77
attrition, war of 25, 43
Austria-Hungary 10, 38, 41, 73, 85

Balkan Wars 9
Beatty, Admiral David 35, 36
Belgium 11, 13
Big Three 78–9
Bolshevik Revolution 59, 63, 72
Bosnian crisis 9
Brest-Litovsk Peace Treaty 63
British Expeditionary Force (BEF) 10, 12, 13, 14, 15
Brusilov Offensive 60
Bulgaria 41, 73, 85

Cambrai, Battle of 49, 56, 68
Central Powers 10, 38, 41
Channel Ports (race to the sea) 15
Churchill, Winston 38, 41, 48
Clemenceau, Georges 77, 79, 86
convoys 54
cross-referencing questions 30–2

Dardanelles 38
Dogger Bank, Battle of 35
dreadnoughts 9, 34, 36

Eastern Front 60
exam structure 4–5

February Revolution 62
Flers, Battle of 48
food shortages 35, 37, 53, 62, 71
Franco-Prussian War 8
Franz Ferdinand, Archduke 8, 9
French, Sir John 12, 41

Gallipoli 38–41
gas 23, 24, 28, 43, 44–6, 69

Haig, Sir Douglas 25, 26, 28, 30, 47, 69
Heligoland Bight, Battle of 35

Hindenburg, Field Marshal Paul von 68, 69, 75
Hipper, Admiral Franz von 36

inference questions 7, 18

Jellicoe, Admiral John Rushworth 36
Joffre, Marshal Joseph-Jacques-Césaire 24
Jutland, Battle of 33, 36–7

Kiel Mutiny 73
Kitchener, Horatio Herbert, Lord 26, 41

League of Nations 79, 82
Lenin, Vladimir Ilich 62, 63
Lloyd George, David 18, 77, 79, 86
Ludendorff, General Erich 37, 68–9, 72
*Lusitania* 53, 65

machine guns 21, 24
Marne, Battle of 14
Masurian Lakes 60, 68, 69
Mexico 66
Moltke, Helmuth von 12, 13
Moroccan crises 9

naval blockade of Germany 33, 35, 37, 68, 70, 71
navies 28, 34–8, 53–5, 73, 83, 84
Neuilly, Treaty of 85
Nicholas II, Tsar 61, 62
NOP (nature, origin, purpose) 6, 50–2
North Sea 35–8

Operation Michael 69, 72

Passchendaele 25, 28–9

Q ships 54

race to the sea 15
Rantzau, Count Ulrich 87
reparations 65, 80
Russia 9, 10, 59, 60–3, 72

Scheer, Admiral Reinhard 36
Schlieffen, Count Alfred von 10–11, 13

Schlieffen Plan 7, 10–13, 14
Serbia 8, 9, 60
Sèvres, Treaty of 85
shell shock 23
socialism 72, 73
Somme, Battle of the 25, 26–7, 47
Spartakus League 74
Spring Offensive 68–9
St Germain, Treaty of 85
Suvla Bay 39, 42
synthesis questions 74–6

tanks 24, 26, 43, 47–9
Tannenberg 60, 68, 69
trench foot 23
trench warfare 16–17, 20–3, 24
  football match 16
Trianon, Treaty of 85
Triple Entente 10, 60
Turkey 38, 41, 73, 85

U-boats 28, 53–5
  unrestricted submarine warfare 37, 59, 65
USA 37, 53, 59, 64–7
utility questions 42, 50–2, 58

Verdun, relief of 25, 26
Versailles, Treaty of 77, 80–2, 84

War Guilt Clause 80
Wilhelm II, Kaiser 8, 9, 33, 73
Wilson, President Woodrow 65, 66, 67, 79
  Fourteen Points 77, 78

Ypres 15, 18, 28–9, 44

Zimmermann telegram 66